Turning | Points
IN WORLD HISTORY

The Enlightenment

Harold Maltz and Miriam Maltz, *Book Editors*

Bruce Glassman, *Vice President*
Bonnie Szumski, *Publisher*
Helen Cothran, *Managing Editor*

GREENHAVEN PRESS
An imprint of Thomson Gale, a part of The Thomson Corporation

THOMSON
———*———™
GALE

Detroit • New York • San Francisco • San Diego • New Haven, Conn.
Waterville, Maine • London • Munich

LIBRARY OF CONGRESS CATALOGING-IN-PUBLICATION DATA

The Enlightenment / Harold and Miriam Maltz, book editors.
    p. cm. — (Turning points in world history)
Includes bibliographical references and index.
ISBN 0-7377-1719-X (alk. paper)
    1. Enlightenment. I. Maltz, Harold. II. Maltz, Miriam. III. Series. IV. Series:
Turning points (Greenhaven Press)
B802.E535 2005
940.2'5—dc22   2004059934

Printed in the United States of America

Contents

Foreword

Certain past events stand out as pivotal, as having effects and outcomes that change the course of history. These events are often referred to as turning points. Historian Louis L. Snyder provides this useful definition:

> A turning point in history is an event, happening, or stage which thrusts the course of historical development into a different direction. By definition a turning point is a great event, but it is even more—a great event with the explosive impact of altering the trend of man's life on the planet.

History's turning points have taken many forms. Some were single, brief, and shattering events with immediate and obvious impact. The invasion of Britain by William the Conqueror in 1066, for example, swiftly transformed that land's political and social institutions and paved the way for the rise of the modern English nation. By contrast, other single events were deemed of minor significance when they occurred, only later recognized as turning points. The assassination of a little-known European nobleman, Archduke Franz Ferdinand, on June 28, 1914, in the Bosnian town of Sarajevo was such an event; only after it touched off a chain reaction of political-military crises that escalated into the global conflict known as World War I did the murder's true significance become evident.

Other crucial turning points occurred not in terms of a few hours, days, months, or even years, but instead as evolutionary developments spanning decades or even centuries. One of the most pivotal turning points in human history, for instance—the development of agriculture, which replaced nomadic hunter-gatherer societies with more permanent settlements—occurred over the course of many generations. Still other great turning points were neither events nor developments, but rather revolutionary new inventions and innovations that significantly altered social customs and ideas, military tactics, home life, the spread of knowledge, and the human condition in general. The developments of writing, gunpowder, the printing press, antibiotics, the electric light, atomic energy, television, and the computer, the last two of which have recently ushered in the world-altering information age, represent only some of these innovative turning points.

Each anthology in the Greenhaven Turning Points in World History series presents a group of essays chosen for their accessibility. The anthology's structure also enhances this accessibility. First, an introductory essay provides a general overview of the principal events and figures involved, placing the topic in its historical context. The essays that follow explore various aspects in more detail, some targeting political trends and consequences, others social, literary, cultural, and/or technological ramifications, and still others pivotal leaders and other influential figures. To aid the reader in choosing the material of immediate interest or need, each essay is introduced by a concise summary of the contributing writer's main themes and insights.

In addition, each volume contains extensive research tools, including a collection of excerpts from primary source documents pertaining to the historical events and figures under discussion. In the anthology on the French Revolution, for example, readers can examine the works of Rousseau, Voltaire, and other writers and thinkers whose championing of human rights helped fuel the French people's growing desire for liberty; the French *Declaration of the Rights of Man and Citizen*, presented to King Louis XVI by the French National Assembly on October 2, 1789; and eyewitness accounts of the attack on the royal palace and the horrors of the Reign of Terror. To guide students interested in pursuing further research on the subject, each volume features an extensive bibliography, which for easy access has been divided into separate sections by topic. Finally, a comprehensive index allows readers to scan and locate content efficiently. Each of the anthologies in the Greenhaven Turning Points in World History series provides students with a complete, detailed, and enlightening examination of a crucial historical watershed.

Introduction: From the Darkness of the Past to the Dawn of the Modern Age

By the mid–seventeenth century, with the dawning of the Enlightenment, the heritage of the medieval church that had exerted such a stranglehold on European minds began to be regarded with hostility and was increasingly undermined. A spirit of questioning and unrelenting critical analysis was initiated, disseminated by Europe's intelligentsia—by the French *philosophes* (popularizers of philosophical and political theories), by British empiricist philosophers (analysts of scientific methodology), and by many other European thinkers. All of these challenged the authority of church and king.

The Spread of Enlightenment Ideas

In the century following 1650, as historian Jonathan I. Israel notes, an educated, virtually classless, intellectual elite arose in the large European cities—among them Paris, London, Amsterdam, Venice, Berlin, and Vienna. This group of intelligentsia was stimulated by the increased number of newspapers and journals published during this period as well as by the monumental intellectual achievement of the age—the seventeen-volume *Encyclopedia* edited by Denis Diderot and Jean Le Rond d'Alembert and published in Paris (1751–1765). Another vital factor in the intellectual fervor of this era were the Parisian salons in which socially prominent and aristocratic women hosted gatherings with the *philosophes* and other European thinkers for free and vigorous debate on the controversial issues of the day. In addition, as Israel observes, European tea- and coffeehouses provided a public space for social interaction and free exchange of ideas among the intellectuals and thinkers who refused to be bound by either censorship or by the formal constraints of king, judiciary, or church. Israel concludes that this public freedom of expression was important in enhancing the influence of the intelligentsia.

The focus of the Enlightenment was France. The *philosophes* disseminated new and radical ideas in numerous journals, widely read by the upper classes, and in a variety of published works, including essays, novels, autobiographies, and contributions to the *Encyclopedia*. Masters of wit, satire, and invective in their writings, the *philosophes* were both popular and influential. In his discussion of Enlightenment thought, scholar Lewis White Beck succinctly describes the contribution of the *philosophes:*

> The Enlightenment in France was the work of highly gifted and courageous writers who, with the exception of [Jean-Jacques] Rousseau, had no profound or original philosophical ideas. Had there been such names as "sociologist," "anthropologist" (in the modern sense), and "intellectual" these would have been the names they might have chosen for themselves. *Les philosophes*—the name under which they are known to history—is not quite correctly translated as "philosophers." The great French dictionary of philosophy [edited by Andre Lalande] defines *philosophes* in this way: "the group of writers who were partisans of reason, light, and tolerance, and more or less hostile to the existing religious institutions."[1]

The *philosophes* attacked traditional beliefs and long-established institutions. Skeptical in their denigration of dogma and superstition, they relied instead on reason. Contemptuous of the ancien régime, or old order, the *philosophes* criticized its rigid hierarchical structure and exposed its corruption. By doing so, they subverted the authority of the Catholic Church and the king. The *philosophes* also denounced injustice. In this respect, they can be regarded as the conscience of their generation. Finally, the *philosophes* affirmed their faith in humanity: They shared a belief in man's innate capacity for reason and an assumption that progress was possible.

Most renowned of the *philosophes* were Charles-Louis de Secondat, known as Montesquieu (1689–1755); Denis Diderot (1713–1784); François-Marie Arouet, known as Voltaire (1694–1778), probably the greatest genius of the age; and Jean-Jacques Rousseau (1712–1778), who was particularly influential on modern political philosophy and education theory. Although the Enlightenment was centered in France, the intellectual ferment that it engendered was by no means confined to one country. On the contrary, it traversed the length and breadth of Europe, albeit in varying degrees of intensity in different countries.

Religious, Scientific, and Political Challenges

The church and the monarchy together formed a nexus of interrelated institutions, equally authoritarian, against which the Enlightenment intelligentsia rebelled. The church was at the center since it claimed to be the guardian of religious doctrine and intellectual truths. The church also endorsed the divine right of kings, the religio-political theory that was used by absolute rulers to validate their authority. The power of both the church and the monarchy was undermined, and their prestige eroded, by several factors.

The *philosophes* and other intellectuals increasingly disputed the church's insistence that it was the sole and supreme arbiter of various claims to knowledge. For example, the great sea voyages of exploration during the seventeenth and eighteenth centuries resulted in amazing scientific discoveries in anthropology, biology, botany, and geography. These and numerous, exciting discoveries in astronomy, medicine, and other fields of burgeoning science taxed the intellectual ingenuity of the church to its very limits. Knowledge that contradicted the authority of the Bible and canonical texts greatly embarrassed the representatives of the church since they were unable to accept it and powerless to censor it. These new discoveries led to intense pressure from scientists for intellectual recognition by the church of their expanding knowledge of the world and the universe. Scientists also demanded acceptance of their empirical principles and methodology.

As the educated classes became increasingly secular, they repudiated the church's claim to intellectual authority as baseless and irrelevant. While the newly prestigious science surged ahead, stimulated by the vitalized intellectual excitement of the age, the church remained mired in fruitless defense of its archaic, immutable teachings. By the time of the Enlightenment, the church was paying a heavy price for its rigorous attempt to control people's minds. To many, the wonders of this world and the marvels of science had become far more fascinating than salvation of their souls in the next world.

The *philosophes* and other thinkers also attacked the political theories that the church had endorsed for centuries—most notably, the divine right of kings. The entrenched authority of the monarch, thus reinforced by the church's approval, had been further augmented by the assumption that the monarch's power was absolute and unlimited. Hence, for centuries, with few and rare exceptions, Europeans had been subjected to the rigors of arbitrary and tyrannical rule at the hands of their monarchs or surrogate rulers, such as barons, petty princes (or princesses), or other nobles.

The *philosophes'* opposition to the theories of divine right and absolute power was stimulated, in part, by the controversial writings of three influential thinkers—British philosophers Thomas Hobbes (1588–1679) and John Locke (1632–1704) and philosophe Jean-Jacques Rousseau. These political theorists analyzed the crucial concept of the social contract and defined it as an implicit agreement between a ruler and his subjects. They contended, moreover, that a ruler's authority, far from being divinely ordained, actually derived its legitimacy from the people governed: that is, a ruler's power depended on the willing consent of those being ruled. It followed that what was given could also be taken away should the ruler fail to fulfill the duties assigned to him or her in the contract. The monarchy, in this context, was in no way to be taken as a license for privilege and the abuse of power. Building on these ideological foundations, the *philosophes* advocated freedom from tyranny and espoused democracy as a viable form of government.

If the monarchy was to survive the attacks of the *philosophes*, it would have to adapt to a new age; for the age of absolutism was rapidly coming to an end. Challenged throughout Enlightenment Europe, absolute monarchies were modified in several countries, giving way to less autocratic rule by benevolent despots—Frederick II of Prussia, Joseph II of Austria, and Catherine II of Russia.

Various other circumstances contributed to the demise of absolutism, though the institution of the monarchy itself continued to survive (as it does in Europe even today in an attenuated form). There already were a number of independent European city-states, such as Geneva, Switzerland, which had long been self-governing, thereby demonstrating their ability to thrive without any direct rule. Moreover, the population expansion that led to the growth of prosperous cities throughout Europe made the monarchy increasingly irrelevant to the cities' inhabitants. The accruing wealth, expanding commerce, and burgeoning power of these cities enabled them to be relatively autonomous, with their own form of self-government, even if they were nominally subject to a sovereign ruler.

In addition, the American Revolution of 1776 resulted in the former British colony becoming an independent nation that flourished without any monarch at all. Even more remarkable for the time, America successfully made the transition to democracy, thereby serving as an example to the world of what the future could hold—freedom from tyranny under a government elected by the people, accountable to the people, and committed to the preservation of "liberty and justice for all."

To sum up, the attacks on entrenched religious authority and established tradition provided the impetus for the gradual emergence of new structures and value systems. The repudiation of the church's teachings by the *philosophes*, by the empiricists, and by other thinkers helped weaken the power of the church, thereby initiating a new era in much of Europe (and America)—one that continued into the nineteenth and twentieth centuries. The clash between religious authority and scientific methodology had a radical impact on the prevailing criteria for defining "truth" and acquiring knowledge. The new scientists insisted on experimentation, observation, and a reliance on empirical data as preconditions necessary to prove untested hypotheses. By doing so, they effectively freed science from the shackles of religion.

At the same time, the theoretical basis of the monarchy was discredited, and the actual power of the monarch was threatened by revolutionary stirrings that intensified in nineteenth-century Europe. Moreover, many of the ideological concepts of democracy were formulated during the Enlightenment, among them the rights of the individual and the rule of law.

The Age of Reason

The Enlightenment is often referred to as the Age of Reason. As many historians have observed, the *philosophes* consciously applied the concept of reason to a critical analysis of the institutions of their society. However, it can be argued that the Enlightenment could more appropriately be termed the Age of Right Reason—of the correct (or right) use of reason, since the *philosophes* were vociferous in denouncing what they regarded as the incorrect (or wrong) use of reason. European theologians and philosophers had, in past centuries, particularly in the early medieval scholastic period, purported to use reason in their speculative arguments about religious and metaphysical topics. But they actually relied heavily on intuition and faith to buttress assertions that seldom, if ever, possessed any scientific validity. Both the *philosophes* and the empiricists totally rejected most theological arguments as invalid, citing them as examples of the wrong use of reason.

Arguably the greatest of the Enlightenment philosophers was Immanuel Kant (1724–1804) of Königsberg, East Prussia, who is considered by many as equal in genius to the ancient Greek philosopher Plato. Even more than the *philosophes* and the empiricists, Kant set out to sweep away the philosophical debris accumulated by centuries of the wrong use of reason. He criticized, brilliantly and succinctly, the excesses of medieval scholasticism and metaphysical philosophy; he devised criteria for avoiding the wrong use of reason; and he formulated rules and guidelines for the right use of reason. Kant argued that reason itself is subject to limitations and should only be used under certain specific conditions—namely, mathematics, science, and empirical investigations. He thereby cleared the way for the philosophers of centuries to come (though not all adhered to his guidelines).

Social historian Thomas Osborne claims that reason is a

definitive characteristic of the Enlightenment:

> What is enlightenment? . . . In its broadest, most banal, sense, the notion refers to the application of reason to human affairs; enlightenment would be the process through which reason was to be applied to all aspects of human existence, above all in the name of freedom. The period of *the* Enlightenment—which usually means the eighteenth-century French Enlightenment—gave birth to the modern human and social sciences and their central ambition; to render freedom into rational form as an ordering principle in society. . . . The great thinkers of the Enlightenment all believed that reason as opposed to superstition or dogma was the one sure basis of a free and just society.[2]

Enlightenment reason was thus not to be used to analyze esoteric metaphysical concepts or to resolve abstruse religious dilemmas. Instead, it was applied to practical problems; it was utilized by the educated classes to consider the controversial issues of their time. The Enlightenment *philosophes* and thinkers regarded reason as the means to achieve a secular kind of salvation, in contrast to earlier Christian philosophers who emphasized religious faith as essential for spiritual salvation.

The term *Enlightenment* encapsulates the age-old image of the light of knowledge illuminating the darkness of ignorance. More specifically, the light envisioned by the *philosophes* is the light of reason. Light has long been an archetypal symbol in Western culture, but nowhere has it been used with more justification than in eighteenth-century Europe, where the Enlightenment stands in dramatic contrast to the medieval world, referred to in its earliest stages as the Dark Ages. Throughout much of European history, the record of human rights and religious toleration was appalling (with the notable exceptions of Britain, Holland, and some advanced city-states): The scene of heretics and witches being burned at the stake was an all too common one. By contrast, Enlightenment writers and thinkers gave voice to a very powerful affirmation of the rights of man (though not always of woman); of freedom of thought and conscience; and of political liberty, democracy, and the rule of law. Norman Hampson expresses the mood of the Enlightenment:

> However uncertain about the long-term future of humanity, educated men had no doubt that they were themselves living in what they described as a *siecle de lumieres*, an *Aufklarung* or an enlightened age. It seemed to them, not without reason, that humanity was at last visibly freeing itself from the prejudices and superstitions that had produced so much blind cruelty in the past.[3]

The Enlightenment is therefore a crucial turning point in European history. In the wake of the Enlightenment the people of Europe became, in general, more secular, more pragmatic, more empirical, and more intolerant of tyranny as they freed themselves from the yoke of the past. Progress on the road to democracy and to religious, intellectual, and political freedom during the nineteenth and twentieth centuries involved a long and arduous struggle with much backsliding. By the twentieth century, however, many European countries had attained the Enlightenment ideals envisioned by the *philosophes* (with the notable exceptions of the totalitarian regimes in central and eastern Europe). Scholar David Williams refers to the Enlightenment as an "unprecedented encounter between political theory and political actuality." He explains: "It was an encounter in which the voices of political modernity could be heard for the first time, and at the beginning of the third millennium their echo has not yet entirely faded."[4] In its ideology—its affirmation of secular humanism, its reliance on scientific methodology, its pursuit of freedom and democracy, and its belief in progress—the Enlightenment thus foreshadowed the modern age.

Notes

1. Lewis White Beck, ed., *Eighteenth-Century Philosophy*. New York: The Free Press, 1966, pp. 8–9.

2. Thomas Osborne, *Aspects of Enlightenment: Social Theory and the Ethics of Truth*. London: University College London Press, 1998, pp. 1–2.

3. Norman Hampson, *The Enlightenment*. London: Penguin, 1968, pp. 150–51.

4. David Williams, ed., *The Enlightenment*. Cambridge, UK: Cambridge University Press, 1999, p. 70.

Chapter 1

The Origins of the Enlightenment

Turning | Points

IN WORLD HISTORY

The Seventeenth-Century Worldview

Norman Hampson

According to Norman Hampson, a British scholar teaching at Manchester University, the seventeenth century provided an intellectual context for understanding the eighteenth-century Enlightenment. In the following article, excerpted from his book, *The Enlightenment*, Hampson shows that the seventeenth century was influenced in turn by previous eras—by the Renaissance and the Reformation, in particular. Its heritage from the past ensured that the authority of the classics and the Bible remained unquestioned. Indeed, many of the classical texts of the ancient world, most notably those of the Greek philosopher Aristotle (384–322 B.C.) were approved by the church so that classical teachings were often grafted onto Christian theology.

Hampson graphically describes the restrictions in time and space that limited the horizons of the seventeenth-century intellectual world, a world darkened by prevailing superstition, fear, and a belief in hell for the sinner. This constricted worldview was only gradually abandoned after the incredible sea voyages of discovery and further eroded by the notable scientific advances that undermined the authority of the church. However, even seventeenth-century scientists were reluctant to repudiate their contemporary worldview, striving initially to reconcile the new knowledge with tradition.

Historians, in their search for origins, always tend to push back the beginning of whatever they are studying. In *The Crisis of European Consciousness* (1935), Paul Hazard sug-

Norman Hampson, *The Enlightenment*. London: Penguin, 1990. Copyright © 1968 by Norman Hampson. All rights reserved. Reproduced by permission of Penguin Books, Ltd.

gested that the first flowering of the Enlightenment should be sought, not in the eighteenth century, but in the second half of the seventeenth. More recently, Christopher Hill, in *The Intellectual Origins of the English Revolution* (1965), argued that, in England at least, attitudes generally attributed to the Enlightenment were widespread in the late sixteenth century. At this rate the Enlightenment looks like linking up with the Renaissance, itself receding in the direction of the twelfth century! This is a useful warning against mechanical attempts to divide historical evolution into self-contained and homogeneous periods. European societies developed at different rates, responding both to national traditions and to the influence of their neighbours; foreign influences varied in direction and extent from one country to another and from one generation to the next; within a given society different elements of the same social class varied in their receptiveness to new ideas and ideas themselves changed more rapidly in some aspects of thought and taste than in others. . . . Without synthesis history disintegrates into its innumerable and individually meaningless atoms. When due allowance has been made for all the exceptions, it is, I think, helpful to regard the seventeenth century as an age which saw a transition from one intellectual climate to another. In order to understand whatever is implied by the Enlightenment, one must consequently first appreciate the assumptions, attitudes and values against which it reacted.

The Seventeenth-Century Worldview

The cultural horizon of most educated men in western Europe in the early seventeenth century was dominated by two almost unchallenged sources of authority: scripture and the classics. Each in its own way perpetuated the idea that civilization had degenerated from a former Golden Age. The most rational preoccupation for contemporary man was, therefore, by the study of the more fortunate ancients to move back towards the kind of society which the latter had known. Recent European movements, the Renaissance and the Reformation, had reinforced this attitude and enhanced the authority of the sacred texts. The Renaissance and the humanist educational movement had been largely based on a revival of Greek and Latin learning. The Reformation had taken the form of a revolt against the Roman Church, accused of having departed from the true faith as revealed in the Bible. Protestant scholars, from [Martin] Luther onwards, therefore stressed the supreme authority of scripture. The Roman Catholics fought back with rival interpretations and by stressing the authority of the Christian Fathers. In this bitter conflict there was no room for the allegorical latitude which some medieval churchmen had permitted themselves in their approach to scripture. The sixteenth century had thus strengthened the reverence with which men approached the texts that enshrined the twin sources of European civilization.

Veneration of the Classics

It is virtually impossible for us today, whose acquaintance with Latin authors is generally limited to the reluctant translation of texts, 'prescribed' for reasons not always obvious, to appreciate the eager veneration with which the sixteenth and seventeenth centuries approached the classics. During the long agony of the Roman Empire these were the brightest lights that shone across the dark seas of ignorance from a more civilized shore. The new confidence with which the men of the Renaissance claimed the kinship of these illustrious ancestors had been a liberating force. The secular attitudes of Greece and Rome, their conception of civic virtue and the life of active public utility was a useful corrective in a society which, officially at least, assumed the wickedness of man, extolled the contemplative life and believed the destiny of nations to be the prerogative of God. A good deal of classical learning, however, was absorbed into an intellectual order that was assumed to reflect the divine purpose—and therefore carried the sanction of the Church behind it. This was especially true of Aristotle who had been, as it were, canonized when his philosophy was grafted on to Christian theology in the middle ages. The Church's approval had been extended in a general sort of way to cover his scientific, as well as his philosophical, ideas. The sixteenth-century radical, eager to move on to new discoveries, was therefore faced by a double barrier: psychologically, it required a bold man to believe that his own reason—for as yet there was little experiment and no conception of the sovereignty of experimental evidence—had penetrated further than that of the Master. In the second place, perseverance in his presumption might cost him the goodwill of a conservative academic 'Establishment' and might bring him under suspicion of heresy. As late as 1636, in Protestant England, archbishop [William] Laud was enforcing the authority of Hippocrates [ancient Greek physician], Galen [ancient Greek physician] and Aristotle. One must not exaggerate this reverence accorded to the ancients; their texts represented no more than human wisdom and it was at least theoretically possible to argue that they had been wrong in matters of detail. Nevertheless the intellectual

The Divine Right of Kings

The concept of absolute monarchy, whereby the king reigned supreme, was reinforced in the seventeenth century by church teaching: According to religious ideology, just as an omnipotent God ruled the cosmos, so the king, God's chosen, ruled his kingdom; the king derived his power and authority, not from his subjects but from God. The significance of absolute monarchy, in the context of the ancien régime, *is explained by historian Walter Oppenheim in the following excerpt.*

Absolute monarchy was an appropriate system of government during a period of history when religion was the strongest influence over people's behaviour and beliefs, and where the only alternatives were worse. However, no king had actually reached the total power advocated by [Jacques] Bossuet and [Thomas] Hobbes. Even in France, at that time regarded as the pinnacle of absolutism, Louis XIV might proclaim proudly that *'L'État c'est moi'* ['The state is me'], but in reality he had to share his power with other individuals and groups, including the nobles, the Church and the *parlements* (courts). Louis XIV, who professed absolutism, was never able or willing to totally suppress them. Instead he and his royal officials had to work alongside them. Even Louis XIV was answerable, not just to God, but to

world which they had created still imposed its perspectives on the learned, whose commitment to the classical viewpoint was in many respects so automatic as to be unconscious.

The Authority of the Bible

However great the authority of classical authors, the one unquestionable voice of knowledge and duty was that of God himself, as recorded in the Bible, and particularly in the Old Testament. Here was contained both the history of the human race and the explanation of the divine purpose. The first chapter of Genesis bolted the door against any optimistic interpretation of human nature or man's prospect of creating a satisfactory society on earth. The early history of all humanity was known, so far as it could ever be known, from the Old Testament account of the events before the Flood.

the traditions and customs of his state, and these he was careful to respect.

During the eighteenth century the Divine Right of Kings, already more a theory justifying absolutism than a reflection of what really happened, became increasingly discredited. Whilst the coronation ceremony was retained everywhere, other practices which symbolised the monarch's divine status fell into disuse. These included the practice of kings claiming to cure disease by touching the afflicted person. Very few kings now believed, and none asserted, that they had been placed on earth by God to rule absolutely. Instead monarchs looked for other ways to justify their power and existence and it was this that led to the idea that royal power was necessary to protect the state and its people. This was not, as Lord Acton [John Emerich Edward Dalberg], the famous nineteenth-century historian claimed, because the monarchs were on the defensive. None ever felt the need to apologise for the power they enjoyed. On the contrary, they were anxious to increase their powers further, and could give good reasons for doing so.

Walter Oppenheim, *Europe and the Enlightened Despots*. London: Hodder & Stoughton, 1990, pp. 2–3.

Thereafter the Jews, the chosen people under the direct guidance of God, had been the teachers of all antiquity; Plato, for example, had been a pupil of Jeremiah in Egypt. The solution to all such human problems as were humanly soluble was therefore to be found in biblical exegesis. Interpretation might be difficult and opinions conflicting, but the only way to certain knowledge was by establishing the exact significance of God's own statement of his will and purpose. To anyone brought up in this tradition, theology was very properly an incomparably more serious study than the gratification of mere curiosity in matters of science or philosophy. . . .

The Seventeenth-Century Universe in Space and Time

As S. Toulmin and J. Goodfield have shown in *The Discovery of Time* (1965), the universe of the early seventeenth century was, by modern standards, extraordinarily circumscribed in space and time. The earth was its centre. In other words, the whole purpose of the cosmos centred upon man, the only rational being on the only inhabited planet. The stars— whether or not they were still believed to be fixed to crystalline spheres—were very near; comets and other such warnings and messengers practically brushed the earth. Man's knowledge of terrestrial geography had been revolutionized in the comparatively recent past and, by the end of the seventeenth century, world maps were tolerably accurate, so far as the great land-masses were concerned, though many Pacific islands were still unknown. Then as now, accounts of voyages of exploration made exciting reading and [Richard] Hakluyt and his fellow-chroniclers commanded a wide public. Such vicarious travel no doubt helped to broaden many European minds, but the full significance of the transoceanic world could not be appreciated until travellers were replaced by residents with the time, interest and ability to investigate newly-discovered civilizations. It was not until towards the end of the seventeenth century that anthropological information was available in sufficient quantity to exercise a marked influence on European ways of thought.

Voyages of discovery led to an impressive knowledge of

coastlines, but in the interior there were enough blank spaces on the maps for tales of monsters to be credible: a unicorn is, after all, scarcely less improbable than a giraffe or a coeclacanth, and our own age has its doubts about the Abominable Snowman. But the greater part of the globe seemed only marginally relevant to the European Christian, heir to the traditions of Israel and the exclusive fraternity of the Church. Beyond Europe lay the old Islamic enemy, the instrument by which God had from time to time chastised his people. Merchants and missionaries were beginning to describe a mighty Chinese Empire far to the East. But the greater part of the extra-European world contained only 'savages' whose conversion was one of the more unexpected duties imposed by the unfolding of the divine purpose. The educated European had therefore virtually no standards of comparison outside his own society and the classical antiquity on which it modelled itself. Little was known of the ancient civilizations of Egypt and Mesopotamia, or of contemporary societies in different parts of the globe, and from the viewpoint of intolerant Christendom such evidence was mainly useful as a warning of the aberrations into which man inevitably fell when bereft of divine guidance.

This circumscribed universe had had a comparatively recent beginning and was hastening towards an even nearer end. The Creation, it was generally agreed—for here Revelation silenced Aristotle and his eternal universe—took place around 4004 B.C. The greater part of the ensuing period was lost to human curiosity, apart from such evidence as was preserved in the Old Testament, 'for all other histories are but late in respect of the sacred story.' Secular texts threw a dim light as far back as 400 B.C. or thereabouts, but the rest was darkness. Large parts of the Christian era itself were scarcely better known, a few facts—or myths—emerging from the shapeless sands of time. Although it was generally regarded as fruitless, if not actually impious, to try to determine when this brief universe would come to its apocalyptic close, there was general agreement that the fatal date could not be far distant. This was a theme that contemporary writers seem to have found particularly moving. For [Sir Walter] Raleigh [seventeenth-century explorer], for example, 'the long day of mankind' was 'drawing fast towards an evening and the world's tragedy and time near at an end.' Sir Thomas Browne [seventeenth-century writer] sounded the same note of pessimistic resignation:

> We cannot hope to live so long in our names, as some have done in their persons, one face of Janus holds no proportion unto the other. 'Tis too late to be ambitious. The great mutations of the world are acted, or time may be too short for our designs.

Even explorer Sir Walter Raleigh subscribed to the seventeenth-century idea that the world was soon to end.

The new telescopes, which had revealed the existence of sunspots, suggested that decay was already well-advanced in the heavens themselves—for scientific evidence can only answer the questions that scientists think fit to ask.

The Afterlife and Superstition

If man's share in the history of the universe, both as individual and as species, seemed incomparably greater than would now be recognized, his narrower horizons offered little for his comfort. Corrupted almost from the beginning of time, his brief sojourn in a vale of tears was a mere prelude to that Last Judgment where many would be called but few chosen. The destiny of the vast majority of mankind was an eternity of torment. Sir Thomas Browne, who seemed reasonably confident that he himself would 'bring up the rear in heaven', regarded this future prospect as the only thing that made earthly existence tolerable. 'Certainly there is no happiness within this circle of flesh, nor is it in the optics of these eyes to behold felicity.' 'Were there not another life that I hope for, all the vanities of this world should not entreat a moment's breath from me: could Death work my belief to imagine I could never die, I would not outlive that very thought.' Others, less sanguine about their more distant prospects, shared his disparaging view of their present existence. Everyday occurrences were in many respects incomprehensible and often regarded as the sinister product of maleficent occult forces. Superstitious fear had spread its poison over Europe since the more rational days of the later middle ages. The sixteenth and early seventeenth centuries were the great age of witchcraft trials; in Languedoc [France] alone, 400 sorcerers were burned in 1577. There were, it is true, some sceptical voices, but they risked accusations of heresy, for to dispute the existence of pacts with the Devil seemed to cast doubt on the existence of the Evil One himself. In 1584 Bishop Jewell preached before Queen Elizabeth that witchcraft had increased enormously in the previous four years. The storms which delayed the return of James I to Scotland a few years later were an obvious product of sorcery for which many were burned. Recurrent outbreaks of plague in England and the frightful destruction of the Thirty Years War in Germany afforded more tangible reminders of the wrath of God and the vulnerability of fallen man, for whatever happened was evidence of the divine scheme. [Jacques] Bossuet [1627–1704] spoke for his generation when he wrote,

> This long sequence of particular causes which make and break empires, depends on the secret commands of divine Providence. . . . What our uncertain councils mistake for chance is a design elaborated in a higher council, in that eternal council which comprises all causes and effects within a single unity. In this way all things work together to the same end and it is because we fail to understand the whole that we see chance and irregularity in particular occurrences. That is why all who govern feel themselves subject to a more powerful force. What they do is always more or less than they intend and their plans never fail to have unforeseen consequences. There is no human force which, despite itself, does not serve other intentions. Only God knows how to make all things subservient to his will.

Even a courtier like [Claude Henri] Saint-Simon, in the eighteenth century, considered that the number of tactical mistakes made by otherwise competent French generals before the battle of Blenheim was explicable only in terms of divine intervention.

It may well be that, for ordinary people, 'this circle of flesh' had more compensations than Sir Thomas Browne was prepared to concede, but as they picked their precarious way through an incomprehensible world, hell gaped literally beneath their feet and their every thought and action was under the scrutiny of a deity more just than merciful, enthroned in a heaven that was very near.

Gradual Erosion of Seventeenth-Century Beliefs

During the seventeenth century these pessimistic certainties were gradually eroded by new knowledge and new ways of looking at experience which brought first doubt and then, gradually, unprecedented optimism concerning the nature of man and his ability to shape his material and social environment to his own convenience. It has often been suggested that advances in science, particularly in astronomy, were the most effective agents of this change and the names of Galileo [Galilei] and [Isaac] Newton have at times been brandished like battle-standards in the Holy War of science against superstition. This is at best a most misleading oversimplification. It would be ridiculous to deny that the new heliocentric theory of the solar system, expounded by [Nicolaus] Copernicus in 1543 and developed by Galileo almost a century later, had far-reaching implications. The question was not merely who revolved around whom, nor were the occasional Old Testament texts that implied a geocentric universe the real crux of the matter. The astronomical argument concerned the relationship between man and nature. If the earth was in fact the centre, then man was the lord of the universe, as the Greeks had assumed and the Jewish-Christian tradition preached. If, on the other hand, the earth was merely one planet orbiting a local star, it was an easy transition to postulate innumerable similar planets scattered throughout the heavens. As astronomical observation and calculation pushed back the limits of space to unimaginable dimensions and revealed myriads of unsuspected stars, the idea of man as a uniquely significant being appeared increasingly presumptuous. The logical corollary to the new astronomy was the publication in 1686 of [Bernard de] Fontenelle's *De la pluralité des mondes* [*On the Multitude of Worlds*].

To consider seventeenth-century science in this light, while not wholly misleading, is nevertheless a modern anachronism. All, or almost all, the cosmologists were sincerely religious men, deeply convinced that their discoveries glorified God by revealing the unsuspected grandeur of his Creation. Galileo, in 1614, published *The Authority of Scripture*, in which he tried to reconcile science with Revelation, and Newton devoted many years to biblical studies.

Attitudes Toward Women: Stereotypes and Superstitions

Phyllis Mack

Various images of women, widespread throughout the seventeenth century and continuing into the eighteenth, are analyzed critically by Phyllis Mack in the following article. Mack is a feminist scholar who teaches at Rutgers University and is acting director of the Rutgers Institute for Research on Women.

Seventeenth-century Europe, dominated by religion, held two opposing views of women—both symbolic. On one hand, women were idealized as holy and pure, like the Virgin Mary; on the other, they were condemned as sinful, passionate, and demonic. More frequently than not, the negative view prevailed. Women were also associated with the moon and the night, and thus with mystery and the forces of darkness, all feared as sinister. These superstitious beliefs led to women being burned as witches.

Even in the eighteenth century, when religious modes of thought were supplanted by more enlightened views and witch hunts ceased, popular stereotypes of women still persisted. As Mack indicates, the myths and misconceptions about women continued to flourish albeit in various permutations and transformations.

The period of European history from the mid–seventeenth to the mid–eighteenth century was dominated by extraordinary events: political and economic upheavals, religious conflict and consolidation, and the intellectual transformation known as the scientific revolution. . . . How did the devel-

Phyllis Mack, "Introduction," *Women and the Enlightenment*, edited by Margaret Hunt. Binghamton, NY: The Haworth Press and the Institute for Research in History, 1984. Copyright © 1984 by The Haworth Press, Inc. All rights reserved. Reproduced by permission.

opment of scientific thought—the replacement of a religious cosmology by a world view that was materialist and secular—affect perceptions about the attributes of gender? And how did the symbols and stereotypes of Womanhood expressed by men . . . affect the self-images and behavior of thoughtful women? . . .

Women in the Seventeenth Century

During the seventeenth century, most [European] men and women sustained their faith in the importance of religious values, if not the validity of particular religious traditions. They also believed that, were the universe ever completely understood, it would reveal itself to be a single, harmonious totality. Their physical and social world was not compartmentalized but full of analogies, so that the movements of the planets, the structure and functions of government and society, and the private realms of emotional life and personal physiology were all linked together in a single cosmic design. Political thinkers wrote about the state as a macrocosm of the family, with the king as father and husband, parliament as the wife, and the populace as obedient children. . . .

These supposed affinities between public and private, and between nature and spirit, also affected perceptions about the attributes of gender. Because a woman menstruated, her nature was viewed as similar to that of the moon and tides, which shared her monthly cycle. And since the moon shone only with the cold, reflected light of the sun, so women were by nature cold, moist and passive. They could also be sinister; just as the moon was linked to night and mystery, so women had a special affinity with the forces of malevolence that lived in darkness; this formed part of the rationale for the predominance of women among those accused of witchcraft. Men, on the other hand, were thought to be like the sun, which radiates life-giving energy. Men belonged to the world of daylight. They were clear-headed, rational, hot and dry. In the seventeenth century babies were washed in salt water at birth to dry out their brains and strengthen their wit.

The main impact of all this symbolic baggage on the lives of actual women was certainly negative. Women were thought

to be unfit for public citizenship or positions of intellectual
eminence; and in fact there was no self-conscious, clear-cut
women's politics in the early modern period. But outside the
natural political order, in the sphere of spirituality or religious
culture—there women *could* be accepted as figures of authority. "Nature hath put a fierceness into the female," wrote a
Puritan pastor.

> . . . therefore the she-bear and the lyoness are the most rag-
> ing and cruel. But grace makes that naturall impotency of the
> woman, turne impotency for God. Their nature, being fear-
> ful, hath ever been proner to superstition. Men's spirits are
> hardier, do not so easily fear Majesty, tremble at judgements,
> beleeve promises, shun sin, love God as women; so that
> when they are in the way, none are better.

And so when women *did* enter the public arena, it was in
their cultural capacity as symbolic figures or—when they
participated in popular disturbances—as vessels of God's
word or vengeance. Women were visible during the seventeenth century not only as witches, but also as visionaries
who were prominent in social and political movements.
Their own writings reflected popular conceptions of femininity as both holy and demonic, but they also used feminine
themes creatively, as in the prophet Mary Cary's vision of an
apocalypse of healthy children, or the visionary Jane Lead's
use of biblical figures as metaphors to comment on the condition of marriage and widowhood.

The symbolic weight of a woman in public was nowhere
better understood or exploited than by Elizabeth I [queen of
England], who sustained national unity around the persona
of Astraea, the Virgin Empress. For even queens did not
leave the domestic, female, spiritual world to act as rational
public citizens. On the contrary; it was in their capacity as
women—irrational, emotional, permeable, and therefore
susceptible to invasion by spiritual forces,—that women were
tolerated as preachers, missionaries and public speakers. And
it was in their capacity as household members that they
worked, carrying on the domestic occupations of medicine,
brewing, manufacturing textiles, farming, or midwifery.

Women in the Eighteenth Century

Eighteenth century writers on science and society demolished most of these ideas about humanity and its relation to the natural order. The philosophes wrote of human nature as a universal category, and of human behavior as susceptible of scientific investigation; that is, conforming to forces of self-interest or environmental influence which paralleled those of motion and gravity in the physical universe. But how did all of this affect their ideas about women? Once the occult affinities between the attributes of the cosmos and those of gender were no longer intellectually credible, what was the effect on perceptions about the nature of Woman and on the self-images of thoughtful women themselves?

We know, for one thing, that the persecution of women as witches was slowly abandoned; in fact both the witch and the prophet came to be viewed with compassion or ridicule as medical phenomena or social rejects. But popular notions about women's dual nature were remarkably resilient during the eighteenth century, even without the buttress of the conception of nature as both benevolent and sinister. Ministers, political theorists and doctors still described women as emotional, passive and permeable, and they still linked women both to the life-giving forces of nature as instruments of moral regeneration (as in the notion of romantic motherhood) and to the forces of anarchy and disorder (as, for example, in the image of Credit-finance as a woman). Certainly the polarities of the virgin/witch myth became less stark, but the ambiguity about the female nature was no less intense, and it was buttressed even more firmly by a physiology which stressed the reciprocal effect of mind and body—women's bodies having a greater sway over their minds than men's.

The Persistence of Attitudes to Women

Given the profound changes in theory and attitude about both humanity and the physical universe during the Enlightenment, why were attitudes about the female nature so persistent? One reason was surely the altered political and religious climate of eighteenth century Europe. During the seventeenth century, feminine symbols and stereotypes had often been linked to myths about the oppressed in general; they served as a catalyst for political opposition and as a justification for political action. Radicals of various sorts and classes spoke of the oppressed and of women in the same breath as the true servants of God; they used the discourse on women as an instrument of challenge as well as an instrument of victimization, to borrow the terminology of Michel Foucault [twentieth-century social philosopher]. (Although to be sure, the challenge was not on behalf of women. If mystics, Puritans and sectarians were identified with Woman as loving and pious, the forces of evil—the aristocracy or the clergy—were also identified with Woman, now defined as greedy, lustful and vain.) As social and political categories became more fluid, so did the categories of gender: Thus Puritan ministers referred to themselves as the breasts of God, mystical writers—both male and female—used metaphors of maternal love to describe their visionary experience, and Quaker prophets, in an effort to express the ecstasy of their reborn condition, actually switched sexes; women announced that they were now men, and men identified themselves, metaphorically at least, as women.

But the political understanding of mystics and religious radicals who evoked the image of the Whore of Babylon [a sinful institution] was very different from that of the eighteenth century writers who depicted Credit as a passionate woman. The eighteenth century discourse on women functioned not as an instrument of challenge, but as a device to impose order on a society in which change was perceived to be at once desirable and threatening. Many writers continued to acknowledge the passion and energy symbolized by Woman as a positive force, but their impulse to control that force was much more urgent than before because of their anxiety to avoid the horrors of religious violence, which they associated with unrestrained, feminine enthusiasm. Jonathan Swift [satirist], for one, linked enthusiasm in its most execrable forms with women; he took particular aim at "Female Priests" or "Quakers who suffer their Women to preach and pray," comparing them to ancient oracular priestesses. . . . How clever of Swift to satirize religious ecstasy while reinforcing prejudices about women's propensity for carnality and invasion by occult forces! By linking religious fanaticism to femininity, Enlightenment thinkers could feel absolved from blame for past excesses and be assured that the seeds of fanaticism would not germinate in the breasts of upstanding male citizens.

The rejection of passionate enthusiasm as neither a socially acceptable nor a spiritually valid mode of behavior is striking in the internal development of English Quakerism during this period, when, because of their desire to become respectable citizens, men and women colluded in the muzzling of prophetic writers and in the restriction of women preachers to a more restrained, less public role within the Quaker community. Working class radicals apparently felt less compunction to avoid identifying with visionary women. The eighteenth century heirs of early Quaker radicalism, and of the early Quakers' emphasis on feminine symbolism and female public leadership, were the Shakers; a movement explicitly and narrowly created by Ann Lee in the interests of the laboring class.

Certainly the anti-clericalism and satirical tone of Enlightenment literature sound more "progressive" to the modern ear than the visionary writing of earlier periods, as do the pleas in many eighteenth century journals for the education of women. To these writers, the term "human being" ostensibly meant one whose development had not been distorted by religious education or corrupt aristocratic taste; but it also meant one whose personality was not distorted by enthusiasm or undue emotion. So in fact, the enlightened view of what constituted virtue may have become less flexible during the eighteenth century, when the ideal, fully developed human being became defined by restraint, rationality, and orientation toward socially useful goals. Such a person was unquestionably male and in the middling or higher ranks of society. According to one modern observer,

> The ideology of progress which was so deeply entrenched in Enlightenment thought meant that the growth of a humane, rational and civilized society could also be seen as a struggle

between the sexes, with men imposing their value systems on women in order to facilitate social progress. Human history, the growth of culture through the domination of nature, was the increasing assertion of masculine ways over irrational, backward-looking women.

Indeed, for many intellectuals, the categories of gender became almost completely polarized during the Enlightenment; thus medical men wrote about masculine Science penetrating passive, feminine Nature, political theorists advocated a style of public thought and action based on reason divorced from passion, and religious thinkers rejected enthusiasm in favor of a "strong, steady, masculine Piety," as Joseph Addison put it in an issue of *The Spectator*. . . .

Middle class women also gained a degree of intellectual emancipation during the Enlightenment—an eighteenth century educated woman might actually earn her own living through writing or journalism. Women produced the majority of all novels published in England in the second half of the century; women also constituted, for the first time in European history, a large segment of the reading public. Given prevalent attitudes toward enthusiasm and the propensity of women to impulsive behavior, some of these enlightened women may have believed . . . that their social and intellectual emancipation was conditional on their ability to divest themselves of "deviant" feminine character traits.

The *Philosophes* Repudiate Medieval Christian Philosophy

Jonathan I. Israel

Jonathan I. Israel, professor in the School of Historical Studies at the Institute for Advanced Studies at Princeton University, is the author of *Radical Enlightenment*, a monumental eight-hundred-page study of the philosophical background to the Enlightenment. Highly acclaimed by influential critics, this cultural history has been called "magnificent" and lauded as "a masterpiece." The following article is taken from the introduction to the book.

Israel uses 1650 as a convenient vantage point from which to consider the schism between two opposing philosophical systems. The first is the inherited medieval Christian philosophy, often termed scholasticism. This philosophy, considered the handmaiden of religion, served to reinforce Christian doctrine. In sharp contrast to religious philosophy is secular philosophy, which emerged in the mid–seventeenth century (in the works of René Descartes, 1596–1650, and Benedictus de Spinoza, 1632–1677) and was disseminated by the *philosophes* in the late seventeenth and eighteenth centuries. Buttressed by the new science and advocating reason, secular philosophy attacked the basic tenets of religion. In the ensuing acrimonious dispute between the two, secular Enlightenment philosophy triumphed as it garnered widespread support among the educated and even the lower classes. Philosophy thus became a powerful force and, reinvigorated, it regained the status that it had once held in ancient Greece.

In his analysis, Israel indicates that the ideological conflict became even more complex, so that much of Europe was soon the scene of a tripartite clash of ideas—not only

Jonathan I. Israel, *Radical Enlightenment: Philosophy and the Making of Modernity 1650–1750*. Oxford, UK: Oxford University Press, 2001. Copyright © 2001 by Jonathan I. Israel. Reproduced by permission of the publisher.

between religious philosophy and enlightened secular views but between moderate and radical Enlightenment thought as well. Alliances were often made between the religious traditionalists and the more moderate philosophers, who joined forces to oppose the radical *philosophes*.

To many a courtier, official, teacher, lawyer, physician, and churchman, philosophy and philosophers seemed to have burst upon the European scene in the late seventeenth century with terrifying force. Countless books reflect the unprecedented and, for some, intoxicating, intellectual and spiritual upheaval of those decades, a vast turbulence in every sphere of knowledge and belief which shook European civilization to its foundations. A sense of shock and acute danger penetrated even the most remote and best defended fastnesses of the west. . . .

During the later Middle Ages and the early modern age down to around 1650, western civilization was based on a largely shared core of faith, tradition, and authority. By contrast, after 1650, everything, no matter how fundamental or deeply rooted, was questioned in the light of philosophical reason and frequently challenged or replaced by startlingly different concepts generated by the New Philosophy and what may still usefully be termed the Scientific Revolution. Admittedly the Reformation had earlier engendered a deep split in western Christendom. But throughout the sixteenth century and the first half of the seventeenth, there was still much, intellectually and spiritually, that the western segments of Christendom shared. Mid-seventeenth-century Europe was still, not just predominantly but overwhelmingly, a culture in which all debates about man, God, and the World which penetrated into the public sphere revolved around 'confessional'—that is Catholic, Lutheran, Reformed (Calvinist), or Anglican issues, and scholars fought above all to establish which confessional bloc possessed a monopoly of truth and a God-given title to authority. It was a civilization in which almost no one challenged the essentials of Christianity or the basic premises of what was taken to be a divinely ordained system of aristocracy, monarchy, land-ownership, and ecclesiastical authority.

By contrast, after 1650, a general process of rationalization and secularization set in which rapidly overthrew theology's age-old hegemony in the world of study, slowly but surely eradicated magic and belief in the supernatural from Europe's intellectual culture, and led a few openly to challenge everything inherited from the past—not just commonly received assumptions about mankind, society, politics, and the cosmos but also the veracity of the Bible and the Christian faith or indeed any faith. Of course, most people at all levels of society were profoundly disquieted by such sweeping intellectual and cultural change and frightened by the upsurge of radical thinking. . . . Whereas before 1650 practically everyone disputed and wrote about confessional differences, subsequently, by the 1680s, it began to be noted by French, German, Dutch, and English writers that confessional conflict, previously at the centre, was increasingly receding to secondary status and that the main issue now was the escalating contest between faith and incredulity. . . .

Popular Culture

It is, furthermore, a drama which profoundly involved the common people, even those who were unschooled and illiterate. What did they know of the Scientific Revolution or the new philosophical ideas, one might well ask? Surely, it is often supposed, there was turmoil on the surface but little change in the minds and outlook of the great majority. But while it is true that the intellectual revolution of the late seventeenth century was primarily a crisis of élites—courtiers, officials, scholars, patricians, and clergy, it was precisely these élites which moulded, supervised, and fixed the contours of popular culture. Consequently, an intellectual crisis of élites quickly made an impact on ordinary men's attitudes too and by no means only the minority of literate artisans and small bourgeoisie. Doubtless some officials, theologians, and academics toyed with trying to confine the more awesome shifts in ideas to the sphere of élite culture so as to preserve intact the existing structures of authority and belief among the common people. After 1650, as those pervaded by the new concepts increasingly doubted the existence of Hell and the reality of eternal torment for the damned, for example, some consideration was given to whether it might be possible to screen such disbelief from the general population. But attempting such wholesale deception would have involved restructuring the entire system of cultural relations between élites and common people on the basis of consciously, systematically, and universally propagated fraud and deceit, scarcely a feasible project.

In practice, ordinary folk could not be shielded from the philosophical revolution transforming the outlook and attitudes of Europe's élites. To many the consequences of this seemed alarming in the extreme. Especially worrying . . . was the growing trend among ordinary folk to mock Holy Scripture, reject Heaven and Hell, doubt the immortality of the soul, and question the existence of Satan, demons, and spirits. If one demands proof that new ideas were rapidly transforming attitudes and beliefs throughout society, such proof was abundantly evident on every side and in every part of Europe. Indeed, surely no other period of European history displays such a profound and decisive shift towards rationalization and secularization at every level as the few decades before Voltaire. 'The triumph of the mechanical philosophy,' it has been rightly asserted, 'meant the end of the animistic conception of the universe [belief that objects have souls] which had constituted the basic rationale for magical thinking.' . . .

If one accepts there is a direct and crucial connection between the intellectual revolution of the late seventeenth century and the wide-ranging social and cultural change in Europe in the period immediately preceding Voltaire, then the implications for the history of Enlightenment thought are far-reaching. There is indeed an urgent need for Enlightenment historians to put much more emphasis on what was happening before and down to the 1740s. Indeed, there is a case for arguing that the most crucial developments were already over by the middle of the eighteenth century. . . .

Most accounts of the European Enlightenment concentrate on developments in only one or two countries, particularly England and France. Although it is often taken for granted that this is where the most important philosophical and scientific developments in the century 1650–1750 took place, there are strong grounds for questioning the validity of such an approach. For the intellectual scenario of the age was extremely wide-ranging and was never confined to just one or two regions. It was, on the contrary, a drama played out from the depths of Spain to Russia and from Scandinavia to Sicily. Its complexity and awesome dynamic force sprang not only from the diversity and incompatibility of the new philosophical and scientific systems themselves but also from the tremendous power of the traditionalist counter-offensive, a veritable 'Counter-Enlightenment' which, as with the Counter-Reformation of the sixteenth century, generated a major reorganization and revitalization of traditional structures of authority, thought, and belief. For the age of confessional antagonism, broadly the period 1520–1650, had equipped Europe's governments, churches, courts, schools, and universities with newly devised or reinforced mechanisms of spiritual and intellectual control which proved extremely effective in tightening the cohesion of society and culture, and strengthening the State and ecclesiastical authority, and therefore represented an accumulation of power and influence which was not going to be lightly abandoned anywhere.

However, even the most assertive and intolerant of these instruments of doctrinal supervision, such as the Calvinist *consistoires* or the Spanish Inquisition, were primarily geared to eradicate theological dissent and were soon partly, if not largely, outflanked and neutralized by the advance of new philosophies and scientific ideas which posed a much tougher problem for ecclesiastical authority to deal with than had religious heresy, especially as it proved difficult to separate what was compatible from what was incompatible with established religious doctrine. Hence, before long, confusion, hesitation, and a rapid fragmentation of ideas prevailed everywhere, even in Rome itself. Furthermore, in the new context, in contrast to the past, none of Europe's rulers, not even the Papacy, could easily decide on, or consistently adopt, a coherent intellectual and spiritual strategy. Opinion was simply too divided for this to be feasible. . . .

The most pressing priority in the new context, it was universally acknowledged, was to overcome the growing fragmentation of ideas and, by means of solid demonstrations and convincing arguments, restore stable and enduring structures of authority, legitimacy, knowledge, and faith. But if the need was obvious, how was it to be met? Without a consensus as to the criteria of truth and legitimacy, without an agreed methodology and principles, the task was impossible. Some progress towards the common goal might be made if leading intellects were less inclined to feud with each other and more unified in their attacks on the Radical Enlightenment; but even this limited goal appeared increasingly unattainable. . . .

Rise of the *Philosophes*

Those who undertook to wrestle with the intellectual dilemmas of the age were labelled by [Christian] Thomasius, using the French term *philosophes.* In the late seventeenth century it was a term just beginning to acquire a new and revolutionary resonance. If philosophy itself was as old as pre-classical Greece—or older—it had assuredly been marginal to the life of society since the advent of the Christian empire in late antiquity, from the time of Constantine the Great [A.D. 306–337] onwards. From then until around 1650, philosophy had remained the modest 'serving-maid', as some called it, of theology and in an essentially ancillary relationship to the other great vocational disciplines, law and medicine. It was only with the intellectual crisis of the late seventeenth century that the old hierarchy of studies, with theology supreme, and philosophy and science her handmaidens, suddenly disintegrated. With this philosophy was released from her previous subordination and became once again an independent force potentially at odds with theology and the Churches. No longer the ancillary of others, philosophers became a new breed, formidably different from the subservient, abstract theoreticians of former times. However unsettling in a society expressly based on authority, tradition, and faith, it was henceforth—at any rate down to the dawn of the nineteenth century—the exponents of philosophy (which then included both theoretical and experimental science), as much as, and eventually even more than, the still strongly entrenched theologians and lawyers, who dominated the intellectual agenda and determined the outcome of controversies. Presenting and popularizing the new findings, concepts, and theories, the *philosophes* . . . suddenly discovered that they too could exert a practical impact in the real world—in ideas in the first place but through ideas also on education, politics, religion, and general culture. Philosophy became not just emancipated but also powerful. This happened . . . because *philosophes* had discovered how to influence debates about education, moral notions, the arts, economic policy, administration, and [life in general]. Even in lands remote from the forefront of intellectual innovation, the power of philosophy in the new context was undeniable. . . .

Hence Europe's war of philosophies during the Early Enlightenment down to 1750 was never confined to the intellectual sphere and was never anywhere a straightforward two-way contest between traditionalists and *moderni*. Rather, the rivalry between moderate mainstream and radical fringe was always as much an integral part of the drama as that between the moderate Enlightenment and conservative opposition. In this triangular battle of ideas what was ultimately at stake was what kind of belief-system should prevail in Europe's politics, social order, and institutions, as well as in high culture and, no less, in popular attitudes.

Of the two rival wings of the European Enlightenment, the moderate mainstream, supported as it was by numerous governments and influential factions in the main Churches, appeared, at least on the surface, much the more powerful tendency. . . . This was the Enlightenment which aspired to conquer ignorance and superstition, establish toleration, and revolutionize ideas, education, and attitudes by means of philosophy but in such a way as to preserve and safeguard what were judged essential elements of the older structures, effecting a viable synthesis of old and new, and of reason and faith. Although down to 1750, in Europe as a whole, the struggle for the middle ground remained inconclusive, much of the European mainstream had, by the 1730s and 1740s, firmly espoused the ideas of [John] Locke and [Isaac] Newton which indeed seemed uniquely attuned and suited to the moderate Enlightenment purpose.

By contrast, the Radical Enlightenment, whether on an atheistic or deistic basis, rejected all compromise with the past and sought to sweep away existing structures entirely, rejecting the Creation as traditionally understood in Judaeo-Christian civilization, and the intervention of a providential God in human affairs, denying the possibility of miracles, and reward and punishment in an afterlife, scorning all forms of ecclesiastical authority, and refusing to accept that there is any God-ordained social hierarchy, concentration of privilege or land-ownership in noble hands, or religious sanction for monarchy. From its origins in the 1650s and 1660s, the philosophical radicalism of the European Early Enlightenment characteristically combined immense reverence for science, and for mathematical logic, with some form of non-providential deism, if not outright materialism and atheism along with unmistakably republican, even democratic tendencies.

Down to the 1750s the principal luminaries of the moderate Enlightenment were uninterruptedly battling on several different fronts simultaneously. Divided among themselves into three main separate factions contending for the middle ground, they were at the same time engaged in fending off traditionalists on one flank and radicals on the other. Hence it became a typical feature of intellectual conflict that moderates endeavoured to shield themselves against conservatives by stressing, even exaggerating, the gulf dividing them from the universally reviled and abhorred radicals while, simultaneously, traditionalists sought a tactical advantage, in their public discourse, by minimizing the gap separating the latter from the moderates as much as possible. . . .

The Collapse of Traditionalism

The cultural and intellectual system prevailing in mid-seventeenth-century Europe, with the partial exception only of England and the United Provinces was—deep confessional divisions notwithstanding—doctrinally coherent, geared to uniformity, authoritarian, and formidably resistant to intellectual innovation and change. As such, it harmonized admirably not only with the dominant ecclesiastical and aristocratic hierarchies presiding over Church and society but also the pervasive princely absolutism of the age. Yet, astonishingly, it was precisely when the monarchical principle was most dominant, in France, Germany, Scandinavia, and Italy alike, that this common European culture . . . first faltered, then rapidly weakened, and finally disintegrated. From the 1650s onwards, first in one land, then another, variants of the New Philosophy breached the defences of authority, tradition, and confessional theology, fragmenting the old edifice of thought at every level from court to university and from pulpit to coffee-shop. . . .

A further factor which greatly contributed to the depth and intensity of the general crisis of the European mind was the susceptibility of all major Churches, and many minor ones, made brittle by internecine wrangling both theological and philosophical, to experience major new and enduring rifts within their own ranks. In effect, practically every Church itself became deeply divided, in part over matters connected with current philosophical and scientific debates, while simultaneously beset by fresh forms of internal theological dissension. Hence philosophy served both to complicate and intensify conflicts between rival theological factions, though in Italy and France it also frequently happened that even priest-professors belonging to the same religious orders took opposite sides in the struggle for and against the 'New Philosophy'. . . .

The European crisis had far-reaching intellectual and religious and also, at least potentially, political implications. [Historian Paul] Hazard has been criticized for giving insufficient emphasis to the political aspects of the 'crisis', that is the reaction against divine-right monarchy and absolutist ideology and the onset of republican political theories linked expressly, or tacitly, to radical philosophy. It has also been suggested that Hazard failed to grasp the extent to which the intellectual legacy of the English Revolution of the 1640s . . . may have served not just as a source of radical ideas for the Radical Enlightenment as a whole, but conceivably, even constituted the ideological driving force of the entire European phenomenon, especially its political and social radicalism.

Although it cannot be said that its political thought was one of its most prominent or developed features, undeniably the Radical Enlightenment was republican, did reject divine-right monarchy, and did evince anti-aristocratic and democratic tendencies. Democratic republicanism was a particularly marked feature of the writings of the Dutch, English, and Italian radicals though it is also encountered, albeit much more faintly, in French and German contexts. However, there is little of a concrete nature to suggest that the continental Radical Enlightenment did in fact principally derive from English influence and example. On the whole, it seems more likely that the phenomenon derives from a broader, international context. . . .

In any case, focusing on national contexts is assuredly the wrong approach to an essentially European phenomenon such as the Radical Enlightenment. The movement or current was an international network bent on far-reaching reform philosophically, socially, ethically, in matters of gender and sexuality, and also politically, drawing inspiration from a wide range of sources and traditions, albeit from the 1660s onwards it evinced a high degree of intellectual cohesion, revolving in particular around [Benedict de] Spinoza [seventeenth-century philosopher] and Spinozism. Given the range of its sources and its widespread impact, as well as an immense anti-radical reaction extending to every corner of Europe, the most essential prerequisite for a balanced view of its origins, development, structure, and reception is to adopt a very broad European view.

Chapter 2

Political Theory and Practice During the Enlightenment

Turning|Points
IN WORLD HISTORY

Locke on the Social Contract

D.J. O'Connor

John Locke (1632–1704) was one of the most renowned of the English philosophers. His political theory, in particular, exerted a formative influence on the *philosophes* of the Enlightenment. In the following essay, scholar D.J. O'Connor, a professor of philosophy who taught in South African and British universities, analyzes Locke's views as expressed in his major work, *Second Treatise of Civil Government*, published in 1690.

In the seventeenth and eighteenth centuries, philosophers investigated mankind's social origins by hypothesizing various stages of human development that culminated in the formation of civilized society. Initially, according to Locke's theory, mankind existed in a "state of nature"—a condition prior to society in which human beings were supposed to have lived free and wild, without law, authority, or government. Locke, in common with Thomas Hobbes (1588–1679) and Jean-Jacques Rousseau (1712–1778), then postulates a theoretical construct to represent a subsequent stage of development—namely, the social contract: This was an agreement by which human beings banded together to form a community, voluntarily surrendering their freedom in exchange for the security of law and order. Mankind's acceptance of a legal and judicial authority via the social contract was a rational alternative to the ever-present threat of anarchy prevalent in the "state of nature." For Locke, another advantage of belonging to society is that individual ownership of property is legitimatized, a principle that is disputed by Rousseau in his version of the social contract.

D.J. O'Connor, *John Locke*. Middlesex, UK: Penguin, 1952. Copyright © 1952 by D.J. O'Connor. Reproduced by permission.

[John] Locke's writing on political subjects is reasonably clear and ingenuous as such books go. He was quite frankly a political apologist who wanted to make clear and justify the theoretical basis of the [English] Revolution of 1688. Thus the *Treatises on Civil Government* are not very different in purpose, though vastly different in value, from political articles in the *New Statesman* and *Nation*. The first *Treatise* is an attack on the theoretical principle behind the misbebaviour of the Stuarts [the royal family], the so-called 'divine right of kings'. This argument has no interest for us to-day, living as we do in an age when monarchy has barely an ornamental function.

On the 'State of Nature' and 'Natural Law'

The second *Treatise* is more important. Locke begins with the origin of society. He postulates what he calls a 'state of nature' and a 'natural law'. The former consists in 'men living together according to reason, without a common superior on earth with authority to judge between them'. Man's liberty in this anarchical condition is limited only by the 'natural law' which Locke rather vaguely equates with reason. He presumably means that the natural law is a moral law self-evident to all rational creatures. Reason tells us that we must strive to preserve out own lives and those of our neighbours and refrain from acting to the detriment of the bodily welfare, liberty or property of others. Every man, in the state of nature, has to be his own policeman, judge, and executioner, and this, of course, has serious practical disadvantages. So men agree to resign certain rights proper to them in the natural state 'by agreeing with other men to join or unite into a community for their comfortable, safe and peaceable living one amongst another', secure against internal and, to a lesser degree, external disorders. In return for this security, 'every man by consenting with others to make one body politic under one government, puts himself under an obligation to every one of that society to submit to the determination of the majority'. If men did not contract to submit to majority rule in this way, no civil society would outlast the first political disagreement among its citizens.

It must be noticed, however, that the only rights resigned

by men on their entry into civil society are those of enforcing the natural law. Political power, which men in society resign to their government, is 'a right of making laws with penalties of death, and consequently all less penalties, for the regulating and preserving of property and of employing the force of the community in the execution of such laws and in the defence of the commonwealth from common injury and all this only for the public good'. All other natural rights are retained by the individual.

Analysis of the Social Contract Theory

Locke's version of the famous 'social contract' theory of the origin of civil government is no more satisfactory than other versions. He seems to regard it both as a factual account of the way in which society originated and as a justification of social obligation. The social contract is an historical event and because of it, we have a duty to society. He realizes that objections can be made to both these points and considers them. To the objection that there is no historical evidence for such a beginning to any civil government, Locke replies that such primitive social origins long antedated any written records. It is, therefore, in no way surprising that there should be no evidence. But this reply, though true, does not meet the real point of the objection: why does Locke hold a not very plausible theory about the origin of society for which no evidence can, in the nature of the case, be expected? I cannot help thinking that Locke was generalizing, though he does not say so, from the examples of the American colonies founded about that time. It was not an uncommon practice to draw up a constitution for such a settlement, as Locke himself had helped to do for Carolina, before any large scale emigration had taken place. It would then be plausible to regard the emigrants as parties to a social contract since they were signifying their acceptance of the new constitution by a voluntary act. Moreover, the theory is an attempt to explain political obligation. Locke wanted to answer the question: what is the ground of our duty to society? The social contract theory does at least stress the important point that political authority depends, in some sense, on the consent of those who are governed.

Locke goes on to discuss the objection that 'all men being born under government, some or other, it is impossible any of them should ever be free and at liberty to unite together and begin a new one, or ever be able to erect a lawful government'. His answer is that being born under a government does not make a man a natural subject of it. 'All men, however born, are free.' At birth, we are in the state of nature; and the social contract can be morally binding only on the actual contracting parties. No man can give away the liberty of another, to choose his own form of government. In this matter, even a son is not bound by his father's choice.

Locke is here making a moral evaluation though he appeals to the legal practice of his time in support of his opinion. It is, however, certainly not supported by present day legal practice. Governments do nowadays 'claim power over the son because of that they had over the father'. . . . But does his 'theory' on the matter amount to no more than a pious sentiment? Perhaps Locke is really saying that a man's political obligations are also moral obligations only if the man himself is a party to the social contract. And indeed it seems reasonable enough to suggest that one man's obligations cannot be created by another man's acts.

Separation of Legislature and Executive

So far Locke's political theory is not very original or very important. But he adds a proposal on the organization of political societies that has had a considerable influence on the development of parliamentary democracies since his time. The legislative power in the state, or the power to make laws, must not be in the hands of the same persons who hold the executive power, or the power of enforcing the laws. If this separation of powers is not ensured by the terms of the constitution, the men who form the government will have the power to exempt themselves from obedience to their own laws and the temptation to use this power will be irresistible. Thus a representative government will degenerate into a tyranny. When Locke wrote, he had in mind the recent Stuart despotism in which the king, the executive power in the land, had tried more than once to dispense with the services of parliament and arrogate its functions to himself. The sharp distinction between legislature and executive which Locke was able to draw owed much to the sharp cleavage between parliament and monarchy which was so prominent a political feature of the Stuart era. In Britain since his time, the decline of the political functions of the monarchy, the advent of party government and the cabinet system and the growing powers of the civil service have done much to blur the distinction which Locke wished to maintain. On the whole, the results have not been so subversive of parliamentary democracy as he anticipated. Nevertheless, the situation in Britain during the second world war provided some evidence in confirmation of his prophecy. The substitution of government by order in council for normal parliamentary legislation was expedient in the circumstances, but it was a mere caricature of democratic procedure. When ministers and their civil servants become in this way the effective rulers of a country there is a coalescence of the legislative and executive functions of government which can easily develop, as Locke foresaw, into a new kind of tyranny.

Locke's recommendations on the separation of political powers were taken more seriously outside his own country. But his influence here has been indirect. The French political writer, [Charles-Louis de] Montesquieu, developed Locke's theory of the separation of powers in his book *De l'Esprit des Lois* [*The Spirit of the Laws*] which was published in 1748. In the form in which it was expounded by Montesquieu, the doctrine of the separation of powers was embodied in the American constitution and has had a considerable influence on the constitutions of republican France and of other states, particularly in South America. The main difference between Locke's version of the doctrine and Montesquieu's is that Montesquieu postulated a division of the functions of the state into legislative, executive, and judiciary, in place of the division into legislative, executive, and federative, proposed by Locke.

One curious feature of Locke's political writing which has been very influential is his theory of property. It was not an entirely original theory but Locke made it famous. He starts from the premise, which is not supported by most legal codes, that a man's own body is his own property. In consequence, 'the labour of his body and the work of his hands we may say are properly his. Whatsoever, then, he removes out of the state that nature hath provided and left it in, he hath mixed his own labour with and joined to it something that is his own, and thereby makes it his property.' It looks as if he should maintain consistently with this, that there are degrees of ownership and the more labour a man 'mixes' with a product of nature, the greater his title to its possession. But this would clearly be an awkward and socially unworkable principle. In fact, Locke's criterion is whether a man by working on a natural product 'removes it out of that common state nature left it in'. Nevertheless men may not accumulate as much property as they can. 'As much as any one can make use of to any advantage of life before it spoils, so much he may by his labour fix a property in; whatever is beyond this is more than his share, and belongs to others.'

Even in a primitive community employing little division of labour, so vague a theory would be a poor guide to a law of property. It is not even easy to be sure what sort of 'theory' Locke supposes it to be. He appeals to 'reason' in support of his view and we must therefore presume that he regards it as in accordance with the 'natural law', and so as embodying a value judgement about the *right* basis for a law of property. It is presumably also a recommendation for an amended use of the word 'property' and its associated terms. But if we try to adopt the usage he recommends, we find it far too imprecise to be of any practical use. It is, perhaps, surprising that so indeterminate a doctrine should have been influential. Yet in the economic writings of Adam Smith and [David] Ricardo, it became the basis for the labour theory of value which stated that the value of any commodity was proportionate to the amount of labour expended in its production. And this in turn developed into the theory of surplus value, one of the basic doctrines of [nineteenth-century] Marxist economics. Locke would no doubt have been very distressed at the use to which his suggestion has been put. For his views on inviolability of property rights were decided even for a member of the English middle class. A government might punish a man by putting him to death but it must not deprive him of any of his property without his consent, 'the preservation of property being the end of government'.

On the Government's Misuse of Power

Locke tells us that a government is a trustee for its citizens with certain powers which they have relinquished to it to ensure their more efficient use. This useful notion that the relationship between the government and the governed should be analogous to that between trustee and beneficiary does something to soften the crudities of the social contract theory and draws attention to the important fact that governments have *duties*. But Locke's political theory gives little detailed guidance on the proper relations of governments and the individual citizen. As long as the government uses its powers for the purposes of its trust, it commands the allegiance of its citizens. It can however be justifiably removed by revolution if it misuses these powers, and Locke discusses the circumstances in which a government can be held to have broken its trust. The conditions permitting revolution, as he describes them, coincide strangely with the conditions leading to the Revolution of 1688. But the problem of the correct balance between the demands of public order and welfare and those of individual liberty, which is so acute to-day, are not discussed. They were not topical in the seventeenth century except in so far as they concerned freedom of religious opinions. And the *Treatises on Civil Government* were intended to be tracts for the times. That their value has outlasted the occasion for which they were written is a measure of the intellectual fertility which characterizes so much of Locke's writing.

Montesquieu: *The Spirit of the Laws*

J.H. Brumfitt

Charles-Louis de Secondat, Baron de Montesquieu (1689–1755), aristocrat and *philosophe*, frequently attended King Louis XV's court and traveled widely throughout Europe, shrewdly observing different societies and governments. His most famous work, *The Spirit of the Laws*, published in 1748, encapsulates the philosophy of the Enlightenment, particularly with respect to politics, law, and morality. This work, highly influential both in the eighteenth century and subsequently, is closely examined by J.H. Brumfitt in the following essay. Brumfitt, professor of French at the University of St. Andrews, Scotland, is a distinguished scholar who has published a number of books on the Enlightenment and French intellectual history and literature.

The Spirit of the Laws was considered an innovative, even revolutionary work in its incisive analysis of society. Montesquieu attempted to identify the specific material and moral conditions that gave rise to the many different legal systems found in various countries throughout history as well as in his time. His aim was to account for the differentiation or relativism of legal codes. He investigated and refined the concept of "natural law"—a set of fundamental, rational, apparently self-evident moral principles. He concluded that even though disparate legal systems were all derived from a single source (natural law), this basic natural law was then filtered through specific political, economic, social, and religious ideologies. The result was a variety of legal formulations, which had previously been attributed to arbitrary factors, such as the whim of rulers.

J.H. Brumfitt, *The French Enlightenment*. New York: Macmillan, 1972. Copyright © 1972 by J.H. Brumfitt. Reproduced by permission of Palgrave Macmillan.

Montesquieu's greatest work finally appeared in 1748. Its impact was summed up at the time by one of the shrewdest of contemporary critics, Baron Friedrich Grimm, when he remarked that it had 'caused a complete revolution in the spirit of the nation'. The claim is perhaps exaggerated, for the royal Government was not won over. . . . In some ways, though, it is an understatement, for Montesquieu's influence rapidly extended beyond the frontiers of his native land: the Scottish Enlightenment would not have been the same without him, nor would the Constitution of the United States of America. The ubiquity of Montesquieu's influence can be measured by the fact that he could include among his fervent admirers men as different as Edmund Burke and Jean-Paul Marat. Clearly *De l'Esprit des lois* was a work of outstanding importance.

Yet the fact that it was admired widely, and by men of such diverse political persuasions, might suggest that its doctrine was not as clear as its author would have wished. . . . Yet to say this is not a criticism of *De l'Esprit des lois* itself. Montesquieu was attempting to lay down the guiding principles for the scientific study of society; he was also, in some measure, trying to describe what society *ought* to be like and, in particular, to outline some of the ways in which he thought a society like his own ought to evolve. His work was written over a period of many years and . . . he often gave himself over to the enthusiasms of the moment. It is hardly surprising that the different parts of his work do not dovetail neatly together and that at times he may be accused of self-contradiction. Yet there are perhaps few works of genius about which similar things could not be said.

Originality of Montesquieu's Analysis

In his Preface, and in the first book of the work itself, Montesquieu tries to elucidate his aims, methods and principles. His most original contribution, here, is his concept of law. 'Laws,' he asserts at the very beginning, 'are the necessary relationships which derive from the nature of things.' It is primarily (though not exclusively) in this scientific sense that he uses the term, and his object, when studying different forms of society, is to show how these relationships arise and are conditioned: to show the 'spirit' behind the laws.

In many ways this implies a complete break with traditional political and legal theory. Philosophical jurists of earlier centuries had evolved the concept of 'natural law'—certain fundamental principles which, in the light of reason and morality, seemed self-evident. Through the theory of the social contract they had sought to anchor all existing civil societies in this bedrock of natural law. Yet (though there are, of course, many partial exceptions to this generalisation) they had regarded the positive laws of these societies as the more or less arbitrary products of chance, custom, the wisdom of enlightened lawgivers, or the whims of capricious tyrants. Montesquieu wishes to replace such an approach with one which one is tempted to describe as 'Newtonian': with a theory of society based on observation and on an explanatory hypothesis which, when it is supported by sufficient weight of evidence, itself becomes a scientific 'law'.

Baron de Montesquieu

'Natural Law' in His Theory

However, what I have just said must immediately be qualified. For though Montesquieu ignores the theory of social contract, and though the concept of natural law is almost absent from those chapters in which he discusses the various forces which determine social structure and legislation, yet he is unwilling to discard the anchor which had done such valuable service. To do so would be to risk shipwreck on the reefs of naked power and self-interest which [Thomas] Hobbes had charted. So Montesquieu returns, initially at any rate, to the safety of natural law. Concepts of justice and injustice, he asserts, precede positive laws, and to deny this would be as absurd as to claim that, before a circle had ever been drawn, all radii were not equal. Among the 'natural laws' to which he immediately draws attention are obedience to the positive laws of one's country, gratitude to one's bene-factors, and submission to the will of God. Others, often even more in line with traditional orthodoxy, are mentioned elsewhere in *De l'Esprit des lois*. Moreover, as well as insisting on these natural laws, Montesquieu also insists on the exis-tence of fundamental human instincts. Of these, a desire for peace and a love of sociability are two of the most important (here again he is seeking to exorcise the spirit of Hobbes). The most basic, however, though it only develops with the dawn of reason, is the instinct of religion.

Of course, Montesquieu is taking care not to offend the orthodox, but other texts show that he is not merely paying lip-service to concepts in which he does not believe. These initial principles suggest that his attitude is that of a Carte-sian rationalist rather than that of a scientific empiricist. In what he has to say about his method of investigation, more-over, he seems to show similar hesitation between the two approaches: 'I first of all examined all mankind . . .' he be-gins, but he continues in a way which suggests that he had already decided exactly what he was looking for: 'I laid down the principles and I saw individual cases conform to them as if of their own accord.' It is not surprising that critics have long argued as to which was his fundamental method. Nor is it surprising that they have come to no agreement, for, as the rest of *De l'Esprit des lois* shows, Montesquieu can, at differ-ent times, be both rationalist and empiricist.

It is an oversimplification, though a very convenient one, to say that Montesquieu the Cartesian is most in evidence in the first thirteen books of *De l'Esprit des lois*, and Mon-tesquieu the empiricist in books XIV to XXV. . . .

Three Types of Government

In the first thirteen books, Montesquieu discusses the main types of government, the principles on which they are based, and the sort of legislation which is appropriate to, and charac-teristic of, each type. For him there are three main types of government: the republican (which may be aristocratic, though more usually he thinks of it as democratic), the monarchical, and the despotic. This distinction is not, in itself, particularly original—indeed, with minor modifications, it goes back to Plato. More original, and more important, is Montesquieu's insistence that to each of these forms of government there corresponds a moral and (as we would say) psychological principle which constitutes the dynamic force behind its actions and behind the actions of its citizens. In the case of the republic, this principle is virtue (a word which in Montesquieu's time contained in its meaning a stronger element of 'manliness' than is generally the case today); in the case of a monarchy, it is *gloire* ('glory', here, is an even more inadequate translation, for *gloire* covers a whole range of emotions: pride, dignity, self-esteem, desire for outward recognition, etc.); in the case of despotism (here there are no semantic difficulties) it is fear.

The modern reader may feel that this is just a little too neat and that Montesquieu's categories show a tendency to impose an *a priori* pattern on social phenomena. Similar doubts may also arise in relation to the chapters which follow, for Montesquieu is capable of making rather hasty generalisations on insufficient evidence and is sometimes tempted to replace a description of what, say, 'despotism' is by a more theoretical reconstruction of what the 'ideal' despotism 'ought' to be. Nevertheless, these books, in which he examines the attitudes of his three types of government to a series of problems such as those of education, sumptuary legislation, war and political liberty, constitute a remarkable achievement. They are rich in examples drawn from a wide range of historical and geographical fields, but they illustrate still more clearly Montesquieu's ability to organise the material he has taken over twenty years to amass. They constitute the first real attempt at sociological classification; in them, the apparent chaos of legislation in different societies is, for the first time, reduced to a pattern which is comprehensible on the basis of a small number of initial assumptions.

Montesquieu's Political Preferences

Yet if Montesquieu's primary aim is to understand the 'spirit of the laws', his investigation is far from being an uncommitted one. The causes of social progress and political liberty, of tolerance and humanity, are ever dear to him. At times, he manifests his sympathies openly, but even when this is not the case, the reader can often sense them. *De l'Esprit des lois* is a work of liberal propaganda as well as social science.

'One cannot speak of these monstrous governments without a shudder,' says Montesquieu in his first chapter on despotism. He later tries to do so, at any rate to the extent of explaining why, in order to survive, despotic governments must be cruel and capricious and must rule through terror. Yet this apparent moderation only makes his condemnation more effective, and hatred of despotism (of which Turkey is his main, though by no means his only, example) is one of the central themes of the whole of *De l'Esprit des lois*.

Democracy and monarchy, on the other hand, both have attractions for him. Like the majority of his contemporaries, he had been nurtured on the heroic legends of the Greek and Roman republics. The ideals of unselfish dedication to the interests of the community, which derive from these examples, are ones of which he approves. . . . He could appear as a good republican not only to many eighteenth-century disciples but also to some twentieth-century critics. Yet the democratic republic he admires, though it may be an ideal, is a distinctly forbidding one. If the citizens govern the state, it, in its turn, carefully controls their education, regulates most aspects of their behaviour and demands rigorous adherence to its standards of 'virtue'. Montesquieu's democracy is a totalitarian democracy. Moreover, it is not even, in the sense in which the term is most frequently used today, 'democratic': the democracies of which he most approves are those ancient republics which divided their citizens into 'classes' and gave greater political power to those of greater wealth and standing: his ideal is far from being an egalitarian one.

Lastly it is not, at any rate as far as the modern world goes, a practical one. The idea of direct democracy derives primarily from the example of the Greek city states, and can only function effectively in societies which, like them, are small enough to permit direct contact between the great majority of the citizens. In most contemporary European states, as Montesquieu later concedes, republican democracy is impossible.

One may doubt, however, whether he was particularly dismayed by this conclusion. For though he certainly admired the republican ideal, he did so, as it were, from a safe distance. By nature, he was not the sort of man either to preach or to practise the code of austere virtue. Compromise, moderation and tolerance were nearer to his heart, and if he felt the need for reform, he was also, as an aristocrat and a *parlementaire*, deeply attached to the political traditions of his native land. For all these reasons it was with monarchy rather than democracy that his real sympathies lay.

Monarchy and Despotism

To those nurtured on more recent political slogans, monarchy and despotism might sound suspiciously like the same thing. But in Montesquieu's eyes they were, in principle at any rate, poles apart. Despotism was the arbitrary rule of a single individual who wielded absolute power over the lives and property of his subjects. Monarchy was also the rule of an individual, but of one who governed through intermediate powers and according to fundamental laws. The basic psychological and moral 'principle' behind despotism was fear; monarchy, on the other hand, was permeated by the spirit of *gloire*.

For Montesquieu these were vital distinctions. Yet he was not unaware of the difficulty of maintaining them in practise, faced with a monarch who wished to become a despot. Louis XIV had gone a long way down that slippery slope. Understandably, Montesquieu was preoccupied with erecting barriers to stop his successors sliding in the same direction. If this could be done, then an ideal balance could be achieved, and the unity and singleness of purpose required of the government of a large state could be combined with the continuity of tradition and with respect for liberty (even, within limits, the liberty of political action) of the individual. In consequence, his discussion of monarchy is not merely a description of such monarchies as exist or have existed. It is also propaganda for the type of monarchy which he believes ought to exist. He entitles one chapter: 'Of the excellence of monarchical government.' Yet this excellence was potential rather than actual, and the subsequent history of his own country was to furnish an outstanding example of the failure to realise this potential.

Not that the French monarchy is his only model. In one of the best known, most influential and longest chapters of his work he discusses the English constitution. Concerned as he was with the need for intermediate bodies and fundamental laws to limit the powers of monarchy, it is hardly surprising that the government of eighteenth-century England had a strong appeal for him. It was not quite so strong as a reading of this famous chapter might suggest, for in writing it, though he does not explicitly say so, Montesquieu was attempting to reveal the ideal potentialities of the English constitution rather than to describe the English political scene as a whole. During his visit to England, he had found much to criticise in the latter, and he voices some of his criticisms in a later chapter of *De l'Esprit des lois*. However, the earlier chapter was the one which attracted most attention and which contains the more important aspects of Montesquieu's own political ideas.

Rousseau's Vision of an Ideal Society

Bertrand Russell

Jean-Jacques Rousseau (1712–1778), generally regarded as the most brilliant and controversial of the *philosophes*, was a prolific writer—the author of numerous works on politics, sociology, and education as well as several novels and an autobiography. Rousseau's most seminal work was *The Social Contract*, published in 1762 (on the same subject discussed by John Locke in the previous century). Rousseau's political thought was undoubtedly influenced by his having been born in the Swiss city of Geneva, which resembled the ancient Greek city-states in being small enough to enable each citizen to participate actively in political affairs. Rousseau's political writings were condemned in 1762 by both the French and the Swiss authorities and, forced to flee to avoid arrest, he spent the next years as an outcast, in constant danger.

Rousseau's political thought is analyzed critically by Bertrand Russell, one of the major British philosophers of the early twentieth century. A fellow of Trinity College, Cambridge, England, Russell published important works on philosophy, politics, mathematics, and the theory of science and was awarded the Nobel Prize for Literature in 1950. The following essay is taken from Russell's renowned study, *A History of Western Philosophy.*

In *The Social Contract*, the fullest expression of his political theory, Rousseau praises liberty, asserting that it is his highest political ideal. He insisted, however, that the individual's absolute—or unlimited—liberty must necessarily be curtailed in the interest of the entire community and all its

Bertrand Russell, *A History of Western Philosophy*. London: Simon and Schuster, 1945, G. Allen and Unwin Ltd, 1946, Readers Union with Allen & Unwin, 1954. Copyright © 1945, renewed 1972 by Bertrand Russell. All rights reserved. Reproduced by permission of Routledge, Taylor & Francis. In the United States by the Bertrand Russell Peace Foundation Ltd.

citizens. He concluded that only if every citizen surrendered completely his individual rights and freedom to the community to which he belonged could equality for all be ensured. The community would thus become an all-powerful body and perform three functions: It would afford security and protection to its members; it would represent the greater good of all; and it would carry out the will of its citizens.

Russell emphasizes that Rousseau repeatedly refers to two important concepts—the "general will" and the "general good." Rousseau regards the community's collective will as the "general will" and maintains that it represents the "general good" or welfare of all citizens. The "general will" should not be equated or identified with the private wishes or individual beliefs of the citizens, as expressed by their voting in an election or referendum, since Rousseau disparages the value of the will of the majority or even unanimity. According to his theory, voters are motivated by their own self-interest rather than by altruism. Thus their votes cannot be considered representative of the "general will," which is directed solely and exclusively toward the "general good." Rousseau's theory of the "general will" is unfortunately open to more sinister interpretations. As Russell points out, the end product of putting Rousseau's theory into practice could well be the totalitarian state, which renders the individual completely powerless and deprives him of the liberty so highly praised by Rousseau.

[Jean-Jacques] Rousseau's political theory is set forth in his *Social Contract*, published in 1762. This book is very different in character from most of his writing; it contains little sentimentality and much close intellectual reasoning. Its doctrines, though they pay lip-service to democracy, tend to the justification of the totalitarian State. But Geneva and antiquity combined to make him prefer the City State to large empires such as those of France and England. On the title-page he calls himself "citizen of Geneva," and in his introductory sentences he says: "As I was born a citizen of a free State, and a member of the Sovereign, I feel that, however feeble the influence of my voice may have been on public affairs, the right of voting on them makes it my duty to study them." There are frequent laudatory references to Sparta as it appears in [ancient Greek biographer] Plutarch's Life of Lycurgus [ruler of Sparta]. He says that democracy is best in small States, aristocracy in middle-sized ones, and monarchy in large ones. But it is to be understood that, in his opinion, small States are preferable, in part because they make democracy more practicable. When he speaks of democracy, he means, as the

John Locke, the seventeenth-century political theorist, provided an earlier treatise on the social contract.

Greeks meant, direct participation of every citizen; representative government he calls "elective aristocracy." Since the former is not possible in a large State, his praise of democracy always implies praise of the City State. This love of the City State is, in my opinion, not sufficiently emphasized in most accounts of Rousseau's political philosophy.

Although the book as a whole is much less rhetorical than most of Rousseau's writing, the first chapter opens with a very forceful piece of rhetoric: "Man is born free, and everywhere he is in chains. One man thinks himself the master of others, but remains more of a slave than they are." Liberty is the nominal goal of Rousseau's thought, but in fact it is equality that he values, and that he seeks to secure even at the expense of liberty.

His conception of the Social Contract seems, at first, analogous to [John] Locke's, but soon shows itself more akin to that of [Thomas] Hobbes. In the development from the state of nature, there comes a time when individuals can no longer maintain themselves in primitive independence; it then becomes necessary to self-preservation that they should unite to form a society. But how can I pledge my liberty without harming my interests? "The problem is to find a form of association which will defend and protect with the whole common force the person and goods of each associate, and in which each, while uniting himself with all, may still obey himself alone, and remain as free as before. This is the fundamental problem of which the Social Contract provides the solution."

The Contract consists in "the total alienation of each associate, together with all his rights, to the whole community; for, in the first place, as each gives himself absolutely, the conditions are the same for all; and this being so, no one has any interest in making them burdensome to others." The alienation is to be without reserve: "If individuals retained certain rights, as there would be no common superior to decide between them and the public, each, being on one point his own judge, would ask to be so on all; the state of nature would thus continue, and the association would necessarily become inoperative or tyrannical."

This implies a complete abrogation of liberty and a complete rejection of the doctrine of the rights of man. It is true that, in a later chapter, there is some softening of this theory. It is there said that, although the social contract gives the body politic absolute power over all its members, nevertheless human beings have natural rights as men. "The sovereign cannot impose upon its subjects any fetters that are useless to the community, nor can it even wish to do so." But the sovereign is the sole judge of what is useful or useless to the community. It is clear that only a very feeble obstacle is thus opposed to collective tyranny.

It should be observed that the "sovereign" means, in Rousseau, not the monarch or the government, but the community in its collective and legislative capacity.

The Social Contract can be stated in the following words: "Each of us puts his person and all his power in common under the supreme direction of the general will, and, in our corporate capacity, we receive each member as an indivisible part of the whole." This act of association creates a moral and collective body, which is called the "State" when passive, the "Sovereign" when active, and a "Power" in relation to other bodies like itself.

The conception of the "general will," which appears in the above wording of the Contract, plays a very important part in Rousseau's system. I shall have more to say about it shortly.

It is argued that the Sovereign need give no guarantees to its subjects, for, since it is formed of the individuals who compose it, it can have no interest contrary to theirs. "The Sovereign, merely by virtue of what it is, is always what it should be." This doctrine is misleading to the reader who does not note Rousseau's somewhat peculiar use of terms. The Sovereign is not the government, which, it is admitted, may be tyrannical; the Sovereign is a more or less metaphysical entity, not fully embodied in any of the visible organs of the State. Its impeccability, therefore, even if admitted, has not the practical consequences that it might be supposed to have.

The will of the Sovereign, which is always right, is the

"general will." Each citizen, *quá* [as] citizen, shares in the general will, but he may also, as an individual, have a particular will running counter to the general will. The Social Contract involves that whoever refuses to obey the general will shall be forced to do so. "This means nothing less than that he will be forced to be free."

This conception of being "forced to be free" is very metaphysical. The general will in the time of Galileo was certainly anti-Copernican; was Galileo [Galilei, 1564–1642, astronomer], "forced to be free" when the Inquisition compelled him to recant? Is even a malefactor "forced to be free" when he is put in prison? Think of Byron's Corsair:

O'er the glad waters of the deep blue sea,
Our thoughts as boundless and our hearts as free.

Would this man be more "free" in a dungeon? . . .

Property

Rousseau has not that profound respect for private property that characterizes Locke and his disciples. "The State, in relation to its members, is master of all their goods." Nor does he believe in division of powers, as preached by Locke and [Charles-Louis de Secondat de] Montesquieu. In this respect, however, as in some others, his later detailed discussions do not wholly agree with his earlier general principles. In Book III, chapter i, he says that the part of the Sovereign is limited to making laws, and that the executive, or government, is an intermediate body set up between the subjects and the Sovereign to secure their mutual correspondence. He goes on to say: "If the Sovereign desires to govern, or the magistrate to give laws, or if the subjects refuse to obey, disorder takes the place of regularity, and . . . the State falls into despotism or anarchy.". . .

The General Will

I come now to the doctrine of the general will, which is both important and obscure. The general will is not identical with the will of the majority, or even with the will of all the citizens. It seems to be conceived as the will belonging to the body politic as such. If we take Hobbes's view, that a civil society is a person, we must suppose it endowed with the attributes of personality, including will. But then we are faced with the difficulty of deciding what are the visible manifestations of this will, and here Rousseau leaves us in the dark. We are told that

Rousseau's Views on Childhood Education

Jean-Jacques Rousseau (1712–1778), arguably the most important of the philosophes, is best known for his political philosophy and his theories on the origin of human society. Closely related to these theories are his views on education, presented in detail in his novel Émile. *In the following brief excerpt, distinguished scholar and author of academic works on French and Italian literature, Julia Conaway Bondanella, sums up the unexpectedly modern concepts of education emphasized by Rousseau in the novel.*

[Rousseau's novel] *Émile*, published in 1762, presents his theory of domestic education. Having established that civilization has corrupted man's original nature, he depicts the development of a child raised in the country and allowed to grow in accord with "the natural progress of the human heart." The objective of education, says Rousseau, should be to form an independent, well-rounded human being who can engage in any vocation. Recognizing that the child has different needs at different stages of development, Rousseau criticizes earlier theorists for treating children like adults and claims that understanding the psychology of children is crucial to a successful educational system. His conception of education rests on the notion that childhood is akin to the state of nature and that parents should not attempt to socialize their children too early. . . .

In the first sentence of *Émile*, [Rousseau] formulates the problem which was to preoccupy all his thought: "Nature has created man to be happy and good, but society depraves him and makes him miserable."

Julia Conaway Bondanella, *Jean-Jacques Rousseau: A Biographical Sketch*, in *Rousseau's Political Writings*, ed. Alan Ritter and Julia Conaway Bondanella. New York: W.W. Norton, 1988, pp. 180–81.

the general will is always right and always tends to the public advantage; but that it does not follow that the deliberations of the people are equally correct, for there is often a great deal of difference between the will of all and the general will. How, then, are we to know what is the general will? There is, in the same chapter, a sort of answer:

"If, when the people, being furnished with adequate information, held its deliberations, the citizens had no communication one with another, the grand total of the small differences would always give the general will, and the decision would always be good."

The conception in Rousseau's mind seems to be this: every man's political opinion is governed by self-interest, but self-interest consists of two parts, one of which is peculiar to the individual, while the other is common to all the members of the community. If the citizens have no opportunity of striking log-rolling bargains with each other, their individual interests, being divergent will cancel out, and there will be left a resultant which will represent their common interest; this resultant is the general will. Perhaps Rousseau's conception might be illustrated by terrestrial gravitation. Every particle in the earth attracts every other particle in the universe towards itself; the air above us attracts us upward while the ground beneath us attracts us downward. But all these "selfish" attractions cancel each other out in so far as they are divergent, and what remains is a resultant attraction towards the centre of the earth. This might be fancifully conceived as the act of the earth considered as a community, and as the expression of its general will.

To say that the general will is always right is only to say that, since it represents what is in common among the self-interests of the various citizens, it must represent the largest collective satisfaction of self-interest possible to the community. This interpretation of Rousseau's meaning seems to accord with his words better than any other that I have been able to think of.

In Rousseau's opinion, what interferes in practice with the expression of the general will is the existence of subordinate associations within the State. Each of these will have its own general will, which may conflict with that of the community as a whole. "It may then be said that there are no longer as many votes as there are men, but only as many as there are associations." This leads to an important consequence: "It is therefore essential, if the general will is to be able to express itself, that there should be no partial society within the State, and that each citizen should think only his own thoughts: which was indeed the sublime and unique system established by the great Lycurgus.". . .

The Totalitarian State

Consider what such a system would involve in practice. The State would have to prohibit churches (except a State Church), political parties, trade-unions, and all other organizations of men with similar economic interests. The result is obviously the Corporate or Totalitarian State, in which the individual citizen is powerless. Rousseau seems to realize that it may be difficult to prohibit all associations, and adds, as an afterthought, that, if there *must* be subordinate associations, then the more there are the better, in order that they may neutralize each other.

When, in a later part of the book, he comes to consider government, he realizes that the executive is inevitably an association having an interest and a general will of its own, which may easily conflict with that of the community. He says that while the government of a large State needs to be stronger than that of a small one, there is also more need of restraining the government by means of the Sovereign. . . . "Everything conspires to take away from a man who is set in authority over others the sense of justice and reason."

Thus in spite of the infallibility of the general will, which is "always constant, unalterable, and pure," all the old problems of eluding tyranny remain. What Rousseau has to say on these problems is either a surreptitious repetition of Montesquieu, or an insistence on the supremacy of the legislature, which, if democratic, is identical with what he calls the Sovereign. The broad general principles with which he starts, and which he presents as if they solved political problems, disappear when he condescends to detailed considerations, towards the solution of which they contribute nothing.

The condemnation of the book by contemporary reactionaries leads a modern reader to expect to find in it a much more sweeping revolutionary doctrine than it in fact contains. We may illustrate this by what is said about democracy. When Rousseau uses this word, he means, as we have already seen, the direct democracy of the ancient City State. This, he points out, can never be completely realized, because the people cannot be always assembled and always occupied with public affairs. "Were there a people of gods, their government would be democratic. So perfect a government is not for men."

What we call democracy he calls elective aristocracy; this, he says, is the best of all governments, but it is not suitable to all countries. The climate must be neither very hot nor very cold; the produce must not much exceed what is necessary, for, where it does, the evil of luxury is inevitable, and it is better that this evil should be confined to a monarch and his Court than diffused throughout the population. In virtue of these limitations, a large field is left for despotic government. Nevertheless his advocacy of democracy, in spite of its limitations, was no doubt one of the things that made the French Government implacably hostile to the book; the other, presumably, was the rejection of the divine right of kings, which is implied in the doctrine of the Social Contract as the origin of government.

The Social Contract became the Bible of most of the leaders in the French Revolution, but no doubt, as is the fate of Bibles, it was not carefully read and was still less understood by many of its disciples. It reintroduced the habit of metaphysical abstractions among the theorists of democracy, and by its doctrine of the general will it made possible the mystic identification of a leader with his people, which has no need of confirmation by so mundane an apparatus as the ballot-box. . . . Its first-fruits in practice were the reign of [Maximilien de] Robespierre [leader in the French Revolution]; the dictatorships of Russia and Germany (especially the latter) are in part an outcome of Rousseau's teaching. What further triumphs the future has to offer to his ghost I do not venture to predict.

The American Colonists: Republicans by Choice

Pauline Maier

Pauline Maier, professor at the University of Massachusetts, has written an insightful study of the political context and ideological implications of the American Revolution: Her book, *From Resistance to Revolution*, traces the various stages of America's transformation from British colony to democratic republic. In the following excerpt, Maier emphasizes that initially, the American colonists were loyal British subjects who were not even seeking independence but were simply protesting various policies and specific abuses (such as excessive customs duty and impressment into the British navy) and demanding that their legitimate grievances be redressed. Only when the British government continued to ignore their demands did protest and resistance become revolution.

Even so, as Maier argues, "revolution did not necessarily imply republicanism"; but the colonists' indictment of King George III evolved into a total repudiation of monarchy as a system of government. Instead, the Americans consciously affirmed democratic principles, deliberately choosing to make their nation a republic based on justice and political liberty. In the context of the Enlightenment, the political ideals embodied by the new American republic replicated those formulated by the European *philosophes* (who repudiated the divine right of kings). American political ideals prefigured in turn those of the French Revolution.

Pauline Maier, *From Resistance to Revolution: Colonial Radicals and the Development of American Opposition to Britain, 1765–1776.* New York: Knopf, 1972. Copyright © 1972 by Pauline Maier. Reproduced by permission of Alfred A. Knopf, a division of Random House, Inc.

The colonists' constitutional arguments, their consistent respect for traditional procedures, even their efforts to contain violence have given later generations an impression that the American Revolution was hardly revolutionary at all. The colonists did not seek change; they set out to defend a constitutional system which had been established, they believed, with the Glorious Revolution of 1688 [the English Revolution]. Here, however, they resembled many other revolutionaries of the seventeenth and eighteenth centuries, who also set out to restore an uncorrupted past. Only when that goal proved unobtainable did contenders establish new regimes that differed profoundly from the past, transforming their own land and sometimes shifting a wider civilization as well.

The colonists sought a past that could not be rewon, if indeed it had ever existed. Hence, to protect liberty as they understood it, the Americans broke off from their Mother Country and undertook one of the earliest modern colonial wars for independence. The movement toward independence constituted the negative phase of the Revolution, a rejection of old and once-revered institutions and ties, which for contemporaries constituted a major upheaval in its own right. It, moreover, opened a second phase of more widespread influence: a revolution in constitutional forms. The achievement of profound political change in the state and federal constitutions of the 1770's and 1780's grew logically out of the popular agitation of the years before independence. The American leaders' concern with peace and good order, their technique of curtailing individual violence by organizing, in effect institutionalizing, mass force—which continued beyond the extra-legal institutions of the 1760's into the committees, conventions, and congresses of the mid-1770's—led naturally toward the re-establishment of regular government. The overall form of these new institutions had also been largely determined by July 1776. Disillusionment with the English constitution and with contemporary British rulers had proceeded simultaneously until it became clear that the new-founded American state should not be modeled after that of England. Instead, it would be what the colonists came to call "republican." This conversion to republicanism transformed [what has been called] "a petty rebellion within the Empire into a symbol for the liberation of all mankind.". . .

The Transition to Republicanism

By 1776 it had become clear not only that the Americans must found their own, independent governments, but also that those new governments would be distinctly different from that of Great Britain. America would be, in short, a republic. The very word inspired confusion, such that John Adams, perhaps the country's most learned student of politics, complained that he "never understood" what a republican government was and believed "no other man ever did or ever will." Compounded from the Latin *res publica*, "republic" meant "the *public good*, or the good of the whole," as Thomas Paine [patriot and writer] explained, "in contradistinction to the despotic form, which makes the good of the sovereign, or of one man, the only object of the government." Technically, then, even England's eighteenth-century constitution could have qualified as "republican"—had it worked in fact as it did in theory, restraining the power of King, nobles, and people, so that the public welfare triumphed over particular interests.

But for Americans and Englishmen of the eighteenth century republicanism was also associated with the Commonwealth period of British history, when for a brief time England was ruled without King or lords; and indeed, "commonwealth" is the closest English equivalent to "republic." "Republic," then, had concrete institutional implications: it suggested a state in which all power flowed from the people, none from inherited title. In this sense, England was hardly republican. . . . The Americans' later conversion to republicanism represented, then, more than a reaffirmation of traditional conceptions of the corporate free state, in which all private interests must be sacrificed for the common good. It meant that the people alone would allocate power. It meant that the United States would have neither legally established nobility nor King.

Revolution did not necessarily imply republicanism. England's Glorious Revolution of 1688 had turned out one monarch [James II] only to establish another [William of

Orange]. Nor did independence imply republicanism. As recently as 1766, when the Portsmouth, New Hampshire, Sons of Liberty mentioned independence (so as to express their "darkest Gloom and horror" at the prospect), that contingency implied for them "erecting an independent Monarchy here in America." A decade later, however, revolution, independence, and republicanism were intimately interwoven causes, and indeed they had developed together. Disillusionment with monarchy was the major component of the new republicanism, and evidence of antimonarchic sentiment began to emerge in the early 1770's, as attitudes toward George III began to change, until gradually all hereditary rule was rejected by the same arguments used against kingship. By the time Thomas Paine took up the cause of republicanism in *Common Sense*, there was little to be said on the subject that had not already been argued in the previous half decade. Both Englishmen and Americans participated in this reappraisal of British government. But since revolution developed only in the colonies, republican theories could be applied only in America. . . .

A Repudiation of Monarchy

By [1774] it was clear to many colonists that the major "error" of England's regime was its retention of monarchy, and of hereditary rule in general. The re-evaluation of monarchy began in earnest soon after George III spurned the London remonstrances and thereby became implicated in the "ministers'" plot. In September 1770, the Massachusetts Assembly heard a sermon on the ninth chapter of Nehemiah:

> Behold, we are Servants this day, and for the Land that thou gavest unto our fathers, to eat the fruit thereof, and the good thereof, behold we are Servants in it. And it yieldeth much increase unto the Kings *whom thou hast set over us because of our Sins:* also they have dominion over our bodies, and over our Cattle at their pleasure and we are in great distress.

The text [it was noted] . . . was "a Sermon in itself." Thereafter, American writers continued to elaborate the argument that kings represented blights, not blessings. Two years before the outbreak of war, readers of the *Massachusetts Spy* were told by "A REPUBLICAN" that "Kings have been a curse to this and every other country where they have gained a footing"; of all men "Kings . . . are the least to be trusted." Unless "under such an *excellent* King as the *present*," he suggested with sarcasm, "every man of sense and independency" would prefer a "well constructed REPUBLIC" to a monarchy. A speaker at the 1775 commencement in Princeton, New Jersey, made the same point by citing all the reigning monarchies—Sweden, Turkey, Russia, Prussia, France, Spain, and Portugal; even England, it seemed, had become "the land of slavery—the school of paricides and the nurse of tyrants." Indeed, the orator concluded, "the history of Kings and Emperors is little more than the history of royal villany. The supreme governor of the universe seems to have set up arbitrary Princes on purpose to shew us the concentrated depravity of the human heart."

The combination of human nature and the "trappings of monarchy," in [John] Milton's phrase, seemed peculiarly suited to produce tyranny. "Kings are but men . . . subject to all the passions of human nature," an article in a 1774 *New London Gazette* pointed out; thus they were "too prompt to grasp at arbitrary power, and to wish to make all things bend and submit to their will and pleasure." Their lofty situation fed this lust, as "Monitor" explained in the January 25, 1776, *New York Journal*. "Their being educated in a taste for luxury, magnificence and pleasure, and surrounded with a great tribe of favourites, flatterers, and sycophants, powerfully inclines them to rapaciousness.". . .

The Evils of Monarchy

Monarchy, in short, was a poor risk. "A good King is a miracle," a writer in the *Pennsylvania Packet* concluded in late 1774; and at the 1775 commencement in Princeton, it was said that only God could be entrusted with kingly power, for "it requires the wisdom, the goodness, and all the other attributes of a Deity to support it." Certainly, public advantages had been won from kings, even aside from the "vast increase of debt and taxes" that the "REPUBLICAN" of 1773 had called the only gift of monarchy. But these "signal benefits" were inadvertent, even "contrary to [the kings'] own intention":

> To John's oppressions, and Henry the Third's weakness, we owe the two great charters. To Henry the Eighth we are indebted for our freedom from the power of the Court of Rome, and the Pope's supremacy. To James and Charles the First we are beholden for the petition of right; And lastly to James the Second's bigotry we must place the settlement of the revolution.

As of 1765, England's post-revolutionary kings, especially the Hanoverians, seemed to offer an exception to the dismal history of royalty; but ten years later it was said that William III could be "censured with as little ceremony as James the First, and his three immediate successors were all of them enemies of the people of England." Even the limited power granted the monarchs after 1688 had proved too much, and they, too, fitted the pattern of English dynastic pretensions as outlined by a writer in 1774. It was rare to find an instance where the Crown descended in a regular manner for more than three generations, he claimed, probably because a dynasty that held the Crown over three successions "increased their power to such a great degree as to be obnoxious to the people, and dangerous to their constitution, rights, and liberties." No longer did it seem fitting to cite the Glorious Revolution as the source of the Hanoverian kings; instead, their common ancestry with the Stuarts was stressed, and ultimately their descent from William the Conqueror, who was, as an article of 1774 said, "a SON OF A WHORE." "A French bastard landing with an armed banditti, and establishing himself king of England against the consent of the natives," Thomas Paine later observed, "is in plain terms a very paltry rascally original." The nefarious tendency of monarchy thus became universal through history; there were no more exceptions.

The whole discussion suggested what Paine made explicit: that it was "the republican and not the monarchical part of the constitution of England which Englishmen glory in, viz. the liberty of choosing an house of commons from out of their own body." The constitution of England was "sickly" only "because monarchy hath poisoned the republic, the crown hath engrossed the commons." For the Americans who were suffering its effects, this illness was above all to be avoided in the future. Joseph Warren [American patriot and writer] wrote Samuel Adams in May 1775 that he hoped never again to have to enter a political war, and for that very end wished all the "seeds of despotism" uprooted from American institutions. In particular, he asked that "the only road to promotion may be through the affection of the people." For the various states that set about "new modelling" their government the most pressing need, it seemed, was the freeing of their institutions from "that worst of plagues, the KING'S EVIL; which disorder," a writer in the *New London Gazette* prayed, ". . . will soon be [extir]pated from this otherwise happy land, and nevermore be suffered to infect it again.". . .

Only the Law Is King

Problems remained to be solved. The meaning as well as forms of American republicanism had to be worked out more fully. The colonists' traditional emphasis upon communal rights had to be reconciled with an emergent concern for individual rights. And indeed, republicanism had yet to be durably established: on into the nineteenth century Americans were haunted by fears that their experiment would fail. By the time the old radical coteries broke up, however, the outline of the new nation was clear. America would be independent of Britain; and her only king, as Paine put it, would be the law. No human monarchy would be installed, for kingship was incompatible with government by law, itself the basis of all political liberty. Americans became republicans not automatically and thoughtlessly, nor for lack of an alternative. They were republicans by conviction and by choice.

A Comparison of the American and French Revolutions

Frederick M. Watkins

The American (1776) and French (1789) revolutions are analyzed by Frederick M. Watkins, scholar and professor at Yale University, in the following extract from his book, *The Age of Ideology: Political Thought, 1750 to the Present.* Comparing the two revolutions, Watkins emphasizes their similarity, for each represented a significant advance in the liberation of mankind. However, the cultural-political histories of these two nations reveal significant differences. Prior to the American Revolution, the colonial social order was relatively stable and homogeneous, enabling the Americans to readily assimilate the philosophy of liberalism. By contrast, France was riven by class hostility and subjected to the oppression of an entrenched aristocracy whose power was reinforced by king and clergy. These factors were initially formidable barriers to the acceptance of liberal ideas.

After the American colonies declared their independence from Britain, a democratic republic was immediately established. Americans then had a period of relative peace, stability, and prosperity in which to resolve their problems. Neither civil strife nor international war disrupted the new nation's growth and progress. America also had the moral support of several foreign allies, including France and Spain.

The situation in France was quite different. Before the revolution, the Estates-General (or national parliament), consisting of three estates—clergy, nobility, and commoners, represented the will of the people; but in order to retain power, the third estate (the middle and lower classes) became increasingly dictatorial. Soon after the revolution, France became involved in two struggles—a civil war between the government and disaffected elements at home and a foreign war against European enemies, who feared that the revolutionary contagion would spread to their own countries. Against all odds, the French under the command of Napoléon Bonaparte conquered much of Europe before being finally defeated. The revolutionary fervor swept across Europe with the advancing French army, and the liberal ideas thus disseminated had a political impact on many European countries.

Few men have ever managed to play an active and significant part in two major revolutions. That most unusual privilege was reserved for Thomas Paine. It was remarkable enough that an Englishman should have turned up in America just in time to become an outstanding figure in the American Revolution. It is still more remarkable to find this same man in Paris, some 20 years later, serving as a member of the National Assembly which accomplished an even greater revolution in the affairs of France. In his second revolutionary venture he was, to be sure, less fortunate than in the first. No word or deed of his had any appreciable impact on French opinion, and by voting against the execution of Louis XVI he even got himself

Thomas Paine

for a time in very serious trouble. Nevertheless, he was and remained an ardent supporter of the new revolutionary movement. His pamphleteering skill enabled him, at an early stage of proceedings, to produce a work, *The Rights of Man*, which immediately gained recognition in the English-speaking world as the ablest and most effective defense of the revolutionary position.

Paine regarded the two revolutions as closely related episodes in a common movement toward the liberation of mankind. His opinion was essentially correct. Both were, to a very large extent, expressions of a common ideology, and their joint example did much to encourage the dissemination of that ideology throughout the Western world. When the French Republic, in 1885, presented the American people with a colossal statue of Liberty Enlightening the World, which now stands in New York harbor, it paid grateful tribute to the common bond uniting the two democracies.

The French and American Revolutions Compared

When the French and American revolutions are closely examined, however, it becomes apparent that there are important differences, as well as likenesses, between the two movements. In America the liberal tradition soon came to be the common sense of the people, a bond of union joining them in a common national purpose; in France the revolution still remains, after nearly 200 years, a controversial issue. French politics, and European politics in general, are marked to this day by ideological cleavages which have no real counterpart in American experience. These differences stem from the distinctive character of European liberalism, as it emerged from the particularly gruelling experience of the French Revolution.

If liberal ideas took hold in America with relative ease, it was because social conditions had always been much freer there than on the continent of Europe. When the English settlers first arrived in the New World, they brought with them many of the traditional class distinctions of the old country. These distinctions did not disappear quickly or completely. Down to the end of the colonial period, for example, the authorities at Harvard and Yale had to face the annual headache of listing the incoming class not by alphabetical but by social precedence. With the single exception of Negro slavery, however, legal and customary restrictions on social mobility were comparatively mild, which meant that the break with Great Britain could be accomplished without any very drastic changes in the established social order. European society, on the contrary, was a complex network of long-established privileges and distinctions. The vocations that a man might follow, the taxes he had to pay, even the religion he might profess, were largely determined by the accident of birth, differing widely from class to class and from region to region. The liberal idea of free competition and of equal rights for all was radically at variance with the existing way of life. Under these circumstances, far more than in America, liberalism was bound to appear as a thoroughgoing social revolution.

Revolutionary Ferment in Eighteenth-Century France

France was the country where discontent with the established order first came to a head. In the eighteenth century the French were the intellectual and cultural leaders of the world, chief exponents of the new current of thought, known as the Enlightenment, that marked the coming of the scientific and industrial revolutions. But France was also, in many ways, a country peculiarly resistant to innovation. Traditional monopolies and other vested interests stood in the way of economic progress. Legal barriers and restrictions inhibited social mobility, and official censorship stood as a constant, if rather ineffective, threat to the free exchange of ideas. The great and increasing privileges of the nobility, including their virtual exemption from taxation, aroused particular resentment at a time when the nation, partly as a consequence of expenses incurred in support of the American Revolution, was rapidly approaching bankruptcy. Of all the countries of Europe, France was the one, therefore, where progressive and liberal ideas came most sharply into conflict with the existing political and social realities. A highly explosive situation was quite clearly in the making.

Under these circumstances, one thing only was lacking for the emergence of a revolutionary ideology; the missing element was democracy. At the time when Paine wrote his *Common Sense*, influential Frenchmen were already fully acquainted with and sympathetic to the theory of liberalism. The philosophical principles of the Enlightenment had given them faith in a happier and more progressive world which would follow automatically upon the liberation of men from undue political restrictions. They also believed that time was inevitably on the side of progress, and that the selfish vested interests now standing in its way would lose out in the long run. What they still lacked was any sort of confidence in the possibility of using democratic means for the attainment of liberal purposes. In America Paine had already recommended that the people should stop appealing to the king and take power into their own hands. This was feasible because the colonists had long had representative institutions of their own, and were in a position to use existing colonial legislatures, and experienced political leaders, as agencies of revolutionary action. In France there were no comparable agencies. Under its absolute monarchy the only established channel for the redressing of grievances was an appeal to the king himself. This long remained the only hope of liberal-minded Frenchmen.

The Revolutionary Crisis

In 1789 affairs took a new and revolutionary turn with the election of the Estates General [parliament]. Bankruptcy had finally forced the king to revive this ancient legislative body, last convened in 1611, in a belated effort to retrieve the situation. Although by this time there was a widespread desire for liberal reforms, the Estates as originally constituted were a most unpromising means of achieving them. They consisted of three separate chambers elected respectively by the clergy, the nobility, and the rest of the population, and the agreement of all three was required for any sort of authoritative action. In view of the prevailing discontent, it was clear from the beginning that radical reformers would win the Third Estate by a large majority. In the other two, however, they could hardly hope for more than a minority position. The nobility and the clergy were the classes, after all, whose privileges were most directly threatened by the rise of liberalism; and even though there were many liberals among them, it was unlikely that either group as a whole would go far in that direction. Thus the only way to make the Estates General serve reformist purposes was to change their essential character. The radical reformers of the Third Estate managed to do just that. By a series of more or less illegal maneuvers, they first arranged to double the size of the popular chamber, and then insisted that all three chambers be merged in a unified National Assembly. The result was to give the French revolutionists, at last, an advantage enjoyed from the beginning by their American predecessors. Secure in their control of a national assembly, they could now if necessary defy the king, and proceed in the name of the people. The stage had been set for a second experiment in revolutionary democracy.

The result was the first great triumph of modern ideology, a triumph which, in its revolutionary consequences, makes the American Revolution seem comparatively tame. As spokesmen for the Third Estate, the revolutionists claimed that they and they alone were genuine representatives of the nation. The progressive philosophy of the Enlightenment gave them confidence in their mission. Believing that the progressive realization of universal welfare and happiness was the predestined outcome of history, and that individual freedom was the necessary and sufficient means to the attainment of that end, they felt that theirs was the cause of reason itself, and that anyone who stood out against them was a blind or selfish defender of indefensible special interests. They therefore proceeded in the name of the people, and with the aid of well-managed demonstrations of mob violence, to crush all opposition. In the National Assembly they pushed through by acclamation a *Declaration of the Rights of Man*, which outlawed at a single stroke the whole complex structure of special privileges, and guaranteed the principle of equal rights for all. This was soon followed by a complete reorganization of local government, by the adoption of a decimal system of weights and measures, and even by the introduction of a new, and short-lived, Revolutionary calendar. Few countries have ever adopted so many drastic changes in so short a time. Here, for the first time in history, the revolutionary force of liberal democracy was demonstrated to the full.

The Breakdown of Consensus

For all its many accomplishments, however, the French Revolution also revealed a crucial weakness, a weakness which has proved to be characteristic of ideological movements in general. The difficulty had to do with the maintenance of consensus.

In America, where the ideological aspect of the Revolution was comparatively weak, this difficulty had not proved to be fatal. Although the movement was at first rejected by a strong loyalist group, their opposition left no lasting scars on the new republic. The break with Great Britain was a shock, no doubt, but it did not involve a complete repudiation of the past. In their colonial legislatures and other organs of local government, the colonists had well-established representative institutions, and had developed respected leaders. These institutions enjoyed a measure of popular acceptance, and these leaders had resources of skill and experience that enabled them to effect the transition to a new order without losing the support of the public. In this they were aided by the fact that the objectives of the Revolution were comparatively moderate, and called for no very drastic changes in the social and economic customs of the community. This made it relatively easy for the revolutionary settlement to gain general acceptance, and for the liberal tradition to become the common sense of the American people.

The French Revolution, on the other hand, enjoyed no like advantages. Absolute monarchy had given the French people and their leaders little experience, even at the local level, with the problems of government. The Estates General, which had never previously met within living memory, was totally new, both to the country at large and to its own members. When it tried, in the unprecedented guise of a sovereign national assembly, to lead the country through the painful process of total revolution, it soon lost contact with public opinion. Rather than abandon its ideological hopes, the declining radical minority kept itself in power by increasingly coercive and unpopular means. Liberalism therefore came to be not, as in America, the common sense of a whole people, but the program of a militant and uncompromising faction. The revolutionists were strong in faith, and accomplished miracles. The price they paid was a crippling rift in the unity of the French people.

The Movement Toward Dictatorship

Even more serious in its political consequences was a difference of opinion that emerged not between the Revolution and its enemies, but among the revolutionists themselves. The issue arose out of the conflict, a conflict with which we are now all too familiar, between dictatorship and representative government. The delegates of the Third Estate were elected by a large majority of the French people, and in the earlier stages of the Revolution they undoubtedly reflected the prevailing state of public opinion. Their representative position became ever more doubtful, however, as the growing radicalism of their measures began to alienate the general public. Many wanted to abide by the increasingly moderate views of their constituents; others, more fanatical in their commitment to the liberal ideology, were so sure they represented the true interests, and therefore the true will, of the people that they were determined to go forward and repress all opposition. The extremists, largely associated with a well-organized body known as the Jacobins, finally gained control of the situation, and kept themselves in power for a while by terroristic means. Although this early experiment in party dictatorship was short-lived, the successors of the Jacobins, down to and including the Emperor Napoleon, were likewise revolutionary extremists who maintained their positions by non-representative means. Thus the French revolutionists, unlike the Americans, failed to associate their version of liberal democracy with any stable and effective form of constitutional government. Many of their outstanding victories were won by dictators, like Robespierre and Napoleon, who purported to rule in the name of the people, but were subject to no genuine form of popular control. This association between democracy and dictatorship has remained as one of the more damaging legacies of the French revolutionary tradition.

Domestic problems were not, however, the only cause of this development; international pressures also were largely responsible for forcing the revolutionary movement along the road to dictatorship. Even in the case of firmly established constitutional governments, a resort to dictatorial measures often occurs in times of serious military crisis. It was therefore peculiarly unfortunate that the new and untried French Republic found itself involved from the very beginning in a desperate military struggle with practically all of its neighbors.

This is, indeed, one of the most striking differences between the American and French revolutions. Although the American colonists had to fight a war against the British, their difficulties were greatly eased by the fact that the rest of the world offered them the advantages of benevolent neutrality, and even of active assistance. The Bourbon monarchies of France and Spain, in particular, welcomed the American Revolution as an opportunity to weaken the rival power of Great Britain. Their intervention brought the war to a successful conclusion, and gave the Americans a generation of uninterrupted peace in which to consolidate their constitutional experiments. In the case of France, however, it was the revolutionists, not their enemies, who were diplomatically isolated. Although the first impulse of the neighboring monarchs, as in the earlier revolutionary crisis, was to profit by the discomfiture of an overly powerful rival, they soon took fright at the subversive implications of the revolutionary movement. The execution of the king and queen of France was especially alarming, and speeded up the movement toward military intervention against the revolutionists. As the French Revolution proceeded, therefore, its supporters had to face the grim prospect of fighting, alone and unaided, two simultaneous wars, a civil war against disaffected elements at home, and a foreign war against the united powers of Europe. This double crisis did much to encourage and justify the Jacobins in their assumption of dictatorial powers. It also committed the French to a policy of endless foreign warfare, first defensive, then aggressive, which culminated in the military dictatorship of Napoleon.

The ensuing conquest of practically all Europe was the first decisive demonstration of the power of modern ideology. Confident of their mission as crusaders for the liberation of mankind, the revolutionary leaders proceeded with unprecedented energy and determination to wipe out all domestic opposition, and to convert the whole French people into an effective fighting force. Against the small professional armies of their enemies they threw the irresistible weight of the first modern mass armies, based on universal conscription. These armies were an incomparable military instrument, but they were also more than that; wherever they went, they carried with them the message and promise of the French Revolution. Through their intervention, sweeping liberal reforms were effected in most of Western Europe, parts of which were directly incorporated in the French Empire, others placed under the control of tributary governments. Liberal-minded elements in the conquered territories welcomed these developments, especially at first, and lent their aid to the forces of occupation. The result was a wholesale sweeping away of traditional restrictions, and a massive liberalization of the political institutions of modern Europe. No subsequent reaction could ever wholly succeed in undoing these accomplishments.

But if the triumph of French arms bore witness to the power of liberalism, the ephemeral quality of their victory also demonstrated the inability of this, as of any pure ideology, to provide a lasting solution to the problems of modern politics. What the revolutionary armies succeeded in doing, indeed, was to export the weaknesses of the French revolutionary movement, along with its strengths, to the whole of continental Europe. People everywhere were attracted initially by the promise and achievements of liberalism. The revolutionary principle of equal rights for all, by releasing creative energies from the frustrations of an outworn political and social system, seemed on first acquaintance to be about to remove all barriers to progress. The speed and extent of the ensuing changes soon led, however, in the occupied territories no less than in France itself, to unexpectedly disruptive and painful consequences, and thus to increasing alienation. Many of the advantages of innovation were swallowed up, moreover, by the exactions [demands] of an aggressive military dictatorship whose war needs called for endless sacrifices of men and money. Pride in the glory of their matchless victories might give the French some compensation for these sacrifices; not so for the conquered peoples newly impressed into the French imperial system. As their hostility increased, the imperial regime became the more oppressive, until it finally collapsed. Abroad as at home, revolutionary liberalism had failed to create an effective political consensus, and dictatorship had proved to be a most inadequate substitute. Such was the outcome of the first great experiment in modern ideology.

Chapter 3

Religion, Secularism, and Science in the Enlightenment

Turning | Points

IN WORLD HISTORY

Science Challenges Religion

Frank E. Manuel

Enlightenment scholar Frank E. Manuel of Brandeis University analyzes the triumph of science over religion in the following essay, taken from his book, *The Age of Reason.* During the eighteenth century, the dominance of religion was gradually superseded by an interest in science on the part of the educated classes. The *philosophes* and their followers increasingly repudiated religious doctrine for failing to conform to either scientific standards or rational principles. Whereas religious disputation circled endlessly in arguments and counterarguments, which proved unsolvable, science was advancing and making exciting progress in many fields, particularly astronomy and cosmology.

Although most of the *philosophes* were not themselves scientists, they were popularizers of science who adopted criteria of scientific methodology from various sources. From the writings of French philosopher and mathematician René Descartes (1596–1650), the *philosophes* learned the method of deduction—deriving knowledge from clear ideas. From the work of English philosopher Francis Bacon (1561–1626), they learned the method of induction—generalizing from the particular, based on experimentation. From the arguments of English philosopher John Locke (1632–1704), they questioned the existence of the soul and therefore denied its ability to discern divinely revealed truths: Instead they argued that all ideas were derived from human experience and thus could be modified or even rejected.

The reading public of Europe [in the eighteenth century] lost interest in theological disputations about religious dogma as they became absorbed in contemplation of [Isaac] Newton's

[1642–1727] world-machine, whose rules of motion both of celestial bodies in the heavens and of objects on earth were translated into mathematical formulae. It was amazing to realize that the whole universe was subject to identical physical laws and that these laws could be expressed in mathematical symbols which no one could deny or about which there could be no substantial difference of opinion. Even the skeptical [philosopher] David Hume (1711–1776) expressed his wonderment at the perfect functioning of this world-machine, subdivided into an infinite number of lesser machines: "All these various machines, and even their most minute parts, are adjusted to each other with an accuracy, which ravishes into admiration all men, who have ever contemplated them."

Contrast Between Scientific and Religious Theories

The theologians of the various Christian churches had always been divided among themselves. The new science gave men a sense of security and finitude because it seemed to produce incontrovertible propositions which would stand impregnable for all time. "Every sect, in whatever sphere, is the rallying-point for doubt and error. Scotist, Thomist, Realist, Nominalist, Papist, Calvinist, Molinist, and Jansenist are only pseudonyms. There are no sects in geometry. . . ." wrote Voltaire in his *Philosophical Dictionary*. Two scientists in different parts of the world, Newton in England and [philosopher Gottfried] Leibniz (1646–1716) in Germany, had simultaneously discovered the calculus through independent ratiocination. Few men dared contradict the Newtonian system once it was published. When an advance was made in physics or mathematics it achieved the status of a generally recognized truth about the world which anyone who had studied the elementary principles of these sciences could comprehend. The theologians of the various Christian sects were eternally denying one another's premises, proving one another's affirmations to be falsehoods, denouncing one another as heretics. The suspicion soon dawned upon inquiring minds that either these theological quibblings were a pack of nonsense, or that they concerned themselves with matters which could not be fathomed and therefore ought to be let alone, or that they were rousing men to shed one another's blood over issues which were intrinsically of no consequence. Science was yielding a regular harvest of new discoveries in every field. Why repeat arguments about theology which were usually circular, were of no avail, never reached a widely accepted conclusion, and only ended in civil wars, massacres, and burnings at the stake?

Science as practiced in the laboratory of the physicist Robert Boyle (1627–1691) or as propounded in the writings of Newton did not in and of itself solve the problems of man's destiny on earth or the mystery of creation. Indeed, many of the fathers of seventeenth-century science accepted traditional religious dogmas along with their scientific view of the physical world after creation. Newton himself was profoundly religious and he wrote a commentary on the Book of Daniel. Some proceeded with their researches and experiments as if the two worlds of science and theology were quite separate and distinct. Many of them acted from conviction; others merely gave lip service to revealed religion to keep out of trouble with the authorities.

Science Undermines Religion

Science, however, was steadfastly undermining the Christian view of the world even though the scientists did not attack the church frontally, continued to render it formal obedience, and received its sacraments. Science as a form of knowledge deflected interest from a striving to comprehend the nature of God and his relationship to man to nonmetaphysical researches which were discovering new laws for the physical universe. The external world became the focus of intellectual interest. Of course there were scientists and laymen who interpreted these laws of nature as the work of Nature's God, men for whom every scientific law was but another proof of the perfect wisdom of God who had created so wonderful a world mechanism. To them, the revelation that the whole universe was subject to an identical set of laws governing motion and gravity served to point up the essential unity of the divine creation. But once they accepted God as an Original

Creator or a Prime Mover the scientists did not have further need for His intervention into the workings of the laws of the universe which were destined to go on functioning in the same way forever. Men inevitably became ever more absorbed in uncovering these secret and rational laws of nature and less and less in the God who had created them. Mediaeval thought had considered excessive preoccupation with any aspect of the physical universe evil because the external world could only be a source of sin. The eighteenth century reversed the emphasis and many intellectuals looked askance upon metaphysical questions as a likely way to fall into nonsense, which in the language of the age was equivalent to evil.

While scientists in their laboratories and mathematicians in their studies did not engage in open warfare with revealed religion, in eighteenth-century France there arose a group of popular philosophers who took it upon themselves to do battle with the church and to proclaim the conflict between science and religion in a truculent manner. With a few exceptions, these *philosophes* were not scientists themselves. They were rather popularizers and transmitters to the literate public of Europe of the scientific ideas of the seventeenth century, primarily those of Isaac Newton, René Descartes (1596–1650), John Locke (1632–1704), and Francis Bacon (1561–1626).

Denis Diderot

Voltaire was the most brilliant wit in the group, and Denis Diderot the man with the greatest capacity to co-ordinate and simplify for a vast body of readers the scientific knowledge of the age. The *Grande Encyclopédie*, edited by Diderot and Jean d'Alembert (1717–1783) and published from 1751 to 1772, was the great common enterprise in which, despite individual differences, all the philosophers co-operated to present Europe with a unified body of knowledge in the new spirit.

Criteria of Scientific Method

These *philosophes* set up criteria for determining truth which by the end of the century were generally accepted by men outside the church. They allowed as truth only those facts and theories which could be arrived at by the employment of a strict rationalist or scientific method. Their basic principles they adopted from two thinkers of the previous age, Descartes and Bacon, both of whom they assimilated despite fundamental divergences between them. The *philosophes* had an oversimplified formulation of the method of science, one hardly adequate in our own day, but it served their purpose.

René Descartes

Descartes had taught them to reason, to deduce knowledge by logical steps from clear and distinct ideas, the best example of which was mathematics. If in any field of knowledge a man could reason from one axiom to another with the certainty of a mathematical demonstration, he was on absolutely secure ground and nobody could doubt his assertions. His original axioms naturally had to be as well founded as his later deductions. "We think," explained Diderot, "that the greatest service to be done to men is to teach them to use their reason, only to hold for truth what they have verified and proved."

Now it was perfectly clear to an eighteenth-century intellectual that theological propositions as well as many of the theories about the origin of kingship were not derived in accordance with the principles of the Cartesian method. While the Christian apologists *appeared* to reason logically from basic premises, they were continually allowing arguments drawn from authority and tradition as embodied in the Bible and other sacred writings to be intermingled with their presentations. Moreover, the primary characteristic of the mathematical spirit, as the *philosophes* understood it, was its emphasis on consistency. After examining the Bible, the *philosophes* came to the conclusion that its revelations lacked this requirement for truth, since there were patent discrepancies between one passage and another. Both Judaic and Christian commentators for centuries had made efforts to conciliate the flagrant contradictions, but when eighteenth-century German Biblical scholars and laymen like Voltaire tackled the same texts they concluded that the conciliations were artificial and preposterous. The spirit of logical mathematical consistency which cannot endure contradiction was a potent weapon in the hands of lay intellectuals who judged the documents of the church by this standard.

Francis Bacon

Even more destructive of accepted religious doctrine was the inductive method [concluding from examples to a general rule] which the French *philosophes* acknowledged they learned from the Elizabethan Francis Bacon. As a matter of fact, laboratory scientists were not much influenced by Bacon's exposition of the experimental method of science. . . . [Still,] the Baconian emphasis on the facts of experience as the source of scientific law became a methodological bludgeon in the hands of the intellectuals, who condemned as superstitions all sorts of explanations about the physical universe sanctified only in patristic [ancient church] and scholastic literature. The Baconian emphasis on the experimental method led the *philosophes* to discredit anything which was not in conformity with normal everyday experience and which could not be examined for truth or falsehood by experience. For them the only kind of reality was objective and scientific, the only phenomena allowable those which could be apprehended by the senses. Miracles failed to meet the crucial test. They were strange effects which could not be accounted for by direct natural causes. The religious explanation of their origin was not in conformity with the facts of experience and the workings of natural law in a world which was rational. Diderot argued:

> You see, once one sets foot in this realm of the supernatural, there are no bounds, one doesn't know where one is going nor what one may meet. Someone affirms that five thousand persons have been fed with five small loaves; this is fine! But to-morrow another will assure you that he fed five thousand people with one small loaf, and the following day a third will have fed five thousand with the wind.

At a time when the churches of Europe recognized the existence of angels and devils the *philosophes* demanded that these beliefs submit themselves to the canons of experience. Since no one could prove their existence from experience, they insisted that they were only figments of the imagination, or fabrications of priests who imposed untruths upon mankind.

John Locke

There was a third set of propositions which fortified the polemics of the French intellectuals against revealed religion, and this was the doctrine of John Locke set forth in the *Essay Concerning Human Understanding* (1690). Along with Newton and Bacon he is one of the seminal thinkers whose writings the *philosophes* imported from England and disseminated throughout Europe. Locke taught that there was nothing in the intellect which had not previously been in the senses, and that the senses received their impressions directly from nature, from the external world. This thesis, in its simplified form, was as revolutionary a doctrine for the study of man in society as Newton's world-machine had been for a comprehension of the physical universe. The Christian view of the world had posited an immortal soul which was given and taken away by God and was the center of conflict between good and evil. This soul of man could grasp divine principles which were absolute truths; it could be moved by divine intervention; unless it were corrupted it recognized the truths of religion and the foundations of authority in the state. But what if there were no soul and man's reason were merely the result of combinations of sensations, as the French philosopher Etienne de Condillac (1715–1780) expounded in the wake of Locke? If all knowledge and the reasoning power itself originated in sensations which were mere reflections of the external world, if they were not God-given, then the absolutes upon which the state and society were presumably based would crumble. Ideas of God, the divine right of kings, immortality, and state authority derived from mere sensory perceptions, nothing more. They were not unalterable. Man-made, they could be modified or abandoned. Though Locke himself never ventured that far, his theory of the source of knowledge led men to question every basic premise of society, to try to find out how many of these ideas, no longer revered as religious absolutes, were actually based on falsehoods inculcated into man and written upon the *tabula rasa*, the clean slate of his mind, after birth.

The intellectuals leveled their guns upon organized state religions which in the first half of the century were still powerful, vital, even controlling forces in men's lives. Unlike most previous critics of the Christian church, the *philosophes* were no mere heretics or deviators from true doctrine. They struck at the very roots of the church. The theological disputations of the sixteenth and the seventeenth centuries were as nothing compared to this battle to the death between the secular intellectuals and the church. It was their avowed purpose to demolish the citadel.

Among intellectuals of this persuasion Christianity came to be regarded as a pernicious plot which had been hatched in order to turn the earth over to the oppressive powers of a priestly class. The annals of Christianity were to them a chronicle of lies and crimes, and the day it was wiped out, the more sanguine philosophers believed, all the ills of suffering humanity would disappear along with it. Those worldly abuses with which the Christian church had become associated historically were judged to be the essence of the faith. The whole of revealed—as contrasted with natural—religion, in any of its forms, was nothing but an absurd imposition upon the ignorant. A French Catholic historian of thought has called this attack on the church the Trial of God, the God of the Protestants as well as the God of the Catholics. No longer did men debate the fine points of theological doctrine or the forms of religious rites; they now questioned the role of God himself. Men wondered whether they lived in a world governed by a God who was watching over their immortal souls or whether they were merely subject to laws of nature which had at some remote time been set into motion by a Prime Mover whom deists chose to call God. Discussions on the existence of God were passionate in the salons of the nobility and the *bourgeoisie* and in the correspondence of intellectuals and kings.

The weapons of assault of the philosophers on Christianity were learning, wit, scorn, humor, and mockery, the exposure of a tawdry reality beneath the veil of false piety. Religion was struck at because it was not rational. Even more, it was attacked as a patent fraud, the artifice of those who controlled the instruments of the cult. Most powerful of the harangues against what Voltaire called the "infamous thing" were those which depicted the thousands upon thousands of victims of intolerance among all the revealed religions of the world. Christianity was judged by simple human standards of good and evil. If its priests were hypocrites who transgressed every tenet of the moral code, if the church in the name of purity of doctrine sanctioned the bloody carnage of fellow Christians, then Christianity, far from being sacred and holy, was a wicked institution which had kept mankind in a terrible thralldom and prevented the attainment of peace, harmony, and progress among the peoples of the earth.

The Triumph of Secularism

Roy Porter

What did the *philosophes* accomplish during the Enlightenment? This question is answered in the following essay by Roy Porter, professor in the social history of medicine at University College, London. Porter is the author of numerous books on social history, medicine, and the Enlightenment.

The *philosophes'* contribution to Enlightenment thought was primarily an intellectual one: Their critical, empirical approach to issues—whether religious, political, or philosophical—assumed that nothing was too sacrosanct to be subjected to their analytical scrutiny. Thus they questioned the age-old teachings and doctrines of the church, which had long gone unchallenged. By doing so, they opened the door for other eighteenth-century Europeans to question religious tenets.

The *philosophes* fostered the spirit of scientific inquiry, so that church dogma was replaced with investigative scientific methods in the fields of geography, cartography (mapmaking), astronomy, politics, and the human sciences. A God-oriented vision of the world was superseded by one with man as its focal point (a system of thought termed humanism). In their efforts to emancipate Europeans' minds from the yoke of the past, the *philosophes* helped bring about the secularization—and the liberalization—of European thought.

Vociferous reactionary ideologues during the 1790s blamed all the evils of the French Revolution, as they saw them, upon the *philosophes*. For [Edmund] Burke, . . . the 'illuminati' had been visionaries drunk upon reason; their spe-

Roy Porter, *The Enlightenment*, 2nd ed. Basingstoke, UK: Palgrave, 2001. Copyright © 2001 by Roy Porter. All rights reserved. Reproduced by permission of Palgrave Macmillan.

ciously attractive, pseudo-humanitarian projects and facile rhetoric had charmed the impressionable, and fatally undermined the *status quo*. The antagonists of the Enlightenment could certainly point to erstwhile *philosophes* who were deeply caught up in French Revolutionary politics. When [Marie-Jean de Caritat de] Condorcet died in the Terror, and the democratic author of *The Age of Reason*, Tom Paine, narrowly escaped with his life, it was easy to imply that radical chickens were finally coming home to roost.

It is by-and-large an idle business to blame or praise the *philosophes* for what happened in 1789 and beyond. In any case, almost all its leaders were by then dead, so we cannot divine their reactions. Erasmus Darwin and other liberal reformers hailed the dawn of the Revolution, but had lost sympathy with it by the time of the execution of Louis XVI and the excesses of the Terror.

Achievements of the *Philosophes*

It is pertinent, however, to ask what the *philosophes* achieved in their own times. Noble measures of reform, stimulated by Enlightenment principles and sometimes guided by enlightened ministers, were passed in many nations: Joseph II's abolition of serfdom in the Austrian Empire is a signal instance. Turgot, a *philosophe*, was appointed by Louis XVI to resolve the crisis of the French finances. He failed; but so would anybody. In England, the new 'free trade' political economy of the Scottish school was applauded, and steadily introduced, by Pitt the Younger and his followers. The utilitarian philosophical radicalism systematized by Jeremy Bentham left its undeniable imprint upon nineteenth-century administrative reform, above all, the radical overhaul of the Poor Law.

It may be hard to find measures advocated by [Charles-Louis de Secondat de] Montesquieu, [Francois-Marie Arouet de] Voltaire, [Denis] Diderot, [or Jean le Rond] d'Alembert, . . . which actually came to pass. Yet that may say less about the irrelevance of the *philosophes*, than about the catastrophic failure of the French monarchy to put its own house in order. In any case, the leaders of the 'High Enlightenment' were not primarily trading in mundane political nostrums; they were more concerned with making palpable hits with their criticism, and with a far more sweeping and imaginative attempt to create a new, more humane, more scientific understanding of man as a social and natural being. They were concerned less with blueprints than with analysis, less with conclusions than with questions. What is the nature of man? What is the basis of morality? Is man a social being or not? Or, as Diderot's final play put the question to man, . . . Is he good? Is he wicked? Diderot's lifework was a whirlwind of questions, doubts and ambiguities which cry out to be labelled quintessentially 'modern'.

How do we know? What is right and wrong? Are we just machines, programmed by inheritance, anatomy or chemistry, or conditioned by the environment? Or, on the other hand, do we have free will? Or, perhaps, do we merely *think* we have free will? Where have we come from? Where are we going? All these questions were asked over and over again, sometimes playfully, sometimes philosophically. What is beyond doubt is that this programme of urgent and ceaseless inquiry into the nature of man and the springs of human action inaugurated by the Enlightenment amounts to a radical rejection of, or at least a distancing from, the standard teachings about man, his duties, and his destiny, which all the Christian churches had been imparting authoritatively, through their creeds and catechisms, down the centuries.

The Secularization of European Thought

Historians differ as to how radical, how applicable, the explicit political programmes of the Enlightenment finally were. What seems clear is that its true radicalism lies in making a break with the Biblical, other-worldly framework for understanding man, society and nature, as revealed in the Scriptures, endorsed by the churches, rationalized in theology, and preached from the pulpit. As late as the close of the seventeenth century, Bishop [Jacques-Benigne] Bossuet, Europe's most eminent historian, could write what he called a *Universal History*, in which he saw the history of mankind opening less than six thousand years earlier, subordinated all human affairs to the Divine Will, and in the process, as Voltaire impishly noted, omitted the Chinese entirely. For Christian history, the proper study for mankind was Providence. Philosophical history, as pioneered by Voltaire, took as its subject by contrast the actions of man in nature and society. [Edward] Gibbon's *Decline and Fall of the Roman Empire* (1776–88) even offered a *natural* history of the Christian religion, interpreted as having progressed in the world from purely natural, or secondary, causes. *Philosophe* history—indeed, its perspectives upon man in general—replaced the divine frame of reference with the human.

The Enlightenment thus decisively launched the secularization of European thought. To say this, is not to claim that the *philosophes* were all atheists or that people thereafter ceased to be religious. Both are manifestly untrue. After all, the reaction against the French Revolution produced powerful evangelical and ecclesiastical revivals all over Europe. But, after the Enlightenment, the Christian religion ceased, once and for all, to preoccupy public culture. The Enlightenment is what sets Dante [Alighieri] and [Desiderius] Erasmus, [Gianlorenzo] Bernini, [Blaise] Pascal, [Jean] Racine and [John] Milton—all great Christian [Renaissance] writers and artists—on one side of the great cultural divide, and [Eugene] Delacroix, [Arthur] Schopenhauer, George Eliot and [Charles Robert] Darwin [of the nineteenth century] on the other. Romanticism, one might suggest, is what is left of the soul when the religion has been drained out of it.

As the Enlightenment gained ground, it spelt the end of public wars of faith, put a stop to witch-persecutions and heretic-burnings, and signalled the demise of magic and astrology, the erosion of the occult, the waning of belief in the literal, physical existence of Heaven and Hell, in the Devil and all his disciples. The supernatural disappeared from public life. To fill the gap, nineteenth-century sentimentality had to endow Nature with its own holiness and invent new traditions, above all, a public show of patriotism. Religion remained, of course, but it gradually lost its props in learning, science, and in the well-stocked imagination. The Enlightenment sapped their credibility.

Scientific Inquiry

All such massive changes did not occur overnight. But they did happen. Why? Certain general forces were evidently at work, for example the success of scientific inquiry. It would be grossly misleading to imply that the new science was involved in a pitched battle against religion. Far from it. Most eighteenth-century scientists were men of piety. But through the eighteenth century the discoveries of science, alongside other forms of investigation, were constantly undermining that unique sense of limited time and particular space which the Biblical story, with its Garden of Eden, and events in Bethlehem, and St Peter's successor installed in Rome, needed for its plausibility. Once intellectuals squarely faced the problems to belief posed by billions of stars occupying infinite space, and millions of years, and countless fossils of extinct creatures, and (no less) the history of man's linguistic, cultural and racial diversity throughout the five continents, Christianity was ever after with its back against the wall, forever trying to accommodate itself to new knowledge. The Enlightenment by contrast eagerly seized upon the excitement of the infinite.

The Media and the Intelligentsia

It must above all be emphasized, however, that the Enlightenment was the era which saw the emergence of a secular intelligentsia large and powerful enough for the first time to challenge the clergy. For centuries the priesthood had commanded the best broadcasting media (churches, pulpits), had monopolized posts in the leading educational establishments (schools, universities, seminaries), and had enjoyed legal privileges over the distribution of information.

This changed. It was during the eighteenth century that substantial bodies of *literati* [educated persons] outside the churches began to make a living out of knowledge and writing. Some earned a crust from Grub Street journalism; a few got very rich on the proceeds of their pens. Voltaire said that in his youth, society had been dominated by the well-born; later it had been taken over by men of letters. Such propagandists exploited such new channels of communication as newspapers and magazines (the *Spectator* might be called a kind of daily secular sermon) and utilized the opportunities offered by public opinion in what [Jurgen] Habermas [twentieth-century social historian] has dubbed the 'public sphere'.

They appealed to an ever-broadening reading public, eager for new forms of writing, such as essays and fiction and biography. In turn, their impact was reinforced by such secular institutions as the reading clubs, academies, and literary and scientific societies mentioned above. The First Estate, the 'Lords Spiritual', was thus challenged by a new body, the 'Fourth Estate' (roughly, the press), in a struggle to win the ear of the 'Second Estate' (the traditional political classes) and the emergent 'Third Estate' (the Commons) [Estates: divisions within French society].

It is not easy to make a balanced assessment of the significance of this shift produced by the Enlightenment through the emergence of a powerful body of *literati*, in other words, the intelligentsia (or what [Samuel] Coleridge neatly called the 'clerisy'). In the early modern centuries when knowledge and opinion were still largely expounded by clergymen who owed formal loyalty to higher authorities, the production of ideas followed orthodox and predictable patterns, as was perhaps appropriate for a relatively stable traditional society. The new intelligentsia by contrast had loyalties which were infinitely more varied. Sometimes they wrote for patrons, or for paymasters. But often they wrote to please themselves, or with a broad sense of communicating to a general paying 'public' out there. And, as writers freed themselves from the fetters which had constrained the clergy, the world of letters became deeply diversified. The multiplication of mouthpieces, each clamouring for attention, matched and enhanced the growing diversity of articulate society at large, as literacy rates improved and more people read pamphlets and newspapers.

The Legacy of the Enlightenment

We might suggest this meant greater independence, for writers and readers alike. Or, in other words, the legacy of the Enlightenment was thus the emancipation of the European mind from the blinkers of dogma. If so, the ultimate impact of the Enlightenment would best be characterized as radical. Yet this is too simple, and doubts arise. Ideas never run far ahead of society. And so much of the daring, innovative thought of the eighteenth century was quickly recycled to become the stock props of the established order of the nineteenth.

The brave new Enlightenment sciences of man—analysing social dynamics, population growth, and wealth creation— became the positivistic 'dismal sciences' which were soon to provide perfect ideological fodder for governments eager to explain why capitalist relations were immutable and in- eluctable, why poverty was the fault of the poor. The chal- lenging psychology of [Etienne Bonnot de] Condillac and [Claude-Adrien] Helvétius, which stated that human beings were pregnant with possibilities, was readily co-opted to en- sure obedience and discipline amongst children at school and adults in the workplace. What had once been the exciting vi- sion of 'man the machine' (free of original sin) became the nightmare reality of factory life in the machine age—or, later, behaviourist conditioning.

The Enlightenment helped to free man from his past. In so doing, it failed to prevent the construction of future cap- tivities. We are still trying to solve the problems of the mod- ern, urban industrial society to which the Enlightenment was midwife. And in our attempts to do so, we largely draw upon the techniques of social analysis, the humanistic values, and the scientific expertise which the *philosophes* generated. We remain today the Enlightenment's children.

The Scientific Method and Its Achievements

Peter Gay

Eighteenth-century science is analyzed by eminent historian Peter Gay in the following extract from his prestigious two-volume study, *The Enlightenment: An Interpretation*. Gay, regarded as one of the leading authorities on eighteenth-century European intellectual history, was professor of history at both Columbia and Yale universities. He has published extensively and received several awards for his works, including the National Book Award.

Although some eighteenth-century scientists regretted the loss of certainty and divine purpose inherent in the prescientific view of nature, most were eager to liberate themselves from centuries-old misconceptions by differentiating between values and facts in their study of nature. Most eighteenth-century scientists also welcomed the new age of science, initiated by the teachings of Isaac Newton (1642–1727) and others.

Eighteenth-century Europeans were awestruck at the unprecedented scientific advances of the age. The *philosophes* regarded science not only as their ally in the struggle against religion and superstition, but as the most remarkable method yet devised for advancing human knowledge. The genius of science lay in its principle of verification whereby hypotheses could be tested, confirmed or rejected, or subjected to further research. The scientific method was thus diametrically opposed to the futile disputations of most theologians and religious philosophers, in which discord reigned supreme: The dogmatic adherents of one school ridiculed and denounced the equally dogmatic followers of other schools; proponents of so-called infallible

Peter Gay, *The Enlightenment: An Interpretation*, vol. 2: *The Science of Freedom*. New York: Alfred A. Knopf, 1969. Copyright © 1966 by Peter Gay. Reproduced by permission of Alfred A. Knopf, a division of Random House, Inc.

truths relied on faith, not on evidence that could be tested.

The *philosophes* were the first to foresee that the principles and methods of science could be applied to extending the knowledge of society in the fields of history, politics, philosophy, and culture. The scientific method became the model for all logical thought. The Scottish philosopher David Hume (1711–1776) spoke for his age when he proclaimed that all the sciences are related to human nature, asserting that the "science of man" is essential to understanding the structure of society.

The irresistible propulsion of modern scientific inquiry was toward positivism [recognizing only observable phenomena] . . . and the clean separation of facts and values, foreshadowed by [Francis] Bacon, implied by [Isaac] Newton, triumphantly announced by [David] Hume, taken for granted by the leading scientists of the late eighteenth century. Scientific thinking exacted the stripping away of theological, metaphysical, aesthetic, and ethical admixtures that had been a constituent part of science since the Greeks; scientific philosophers of the eighteenth century, with justice, treated these admixtures as impurities, as survivals from earlier stages of consciousness. Every scientific discovery weakened the hold of theological explanation, metaphysical entities, and aesthetic considerations: the orbits of planets were neither beautiful nor ugly; the law of gravitation was neither cruel nor kind; observed irregularities in the skies proved nothing about divine activity. And every improvement in scientific terminology or mathematical formulation further liberated scientists from old anthropomorphic conceptions of the world and reduced to irrelevance many of the old questions that philosophers had addressed to nature.

It was an exhilarating development. After a millennium of the reign of fancy, the reign of fact was at hand; but, as the philosophes' treatment of nature shows, it was a confusing and at times frightening development as well. Nature had always been a word rich in comforting associations, a profuse, almost inexhaustible metaphor, and the philosophes were reluctant to surrender all these comforts without a struggle. In the age of the Enlightenment, therefore, nature continued to supply norms for beauty and standards for conduct—at least to some philosophes; and the philosophes continued to treat nature rhetorically as a bountiful mother, a treasure house lying open to be raided, a servant waiting for orders, a treacherous opponent requiring constant vigilance. The deists [believers in a God known through reason] admired nature as a storehouse of lessons and evidence of divine skill; the materi-

The *Encyclopedia* Advances Knowledge

The Encyclopedia, *edited by the French* philosophe *Denis Diderot (1713–1784) and others, has been praised by historians as the most ambitious and important intellectual project of the Enlightenment. Attesting to the era's emphasis on knowledge, it contained the* philosophes' *rationalist approach, severe criticism of religion, liberal political views, and advanced scientific thought, in addition to a wide variety of other topics. In the following excerpt from his collection of readings in Enlightenment political thought, editor David Williams, eminent scholar in French literature and thought, describes the publication history of the* Encyclopedia.

In 1746 [Denis] Diderot was approached by a [Parisian] publisher . . . to produce a translation of Ephraim Chambers' *Cyclopedia*. This commission was to develop into his most ambitious work, *The Encyclopedia, or rational dictionary of the sciences, arts and crafts*, and in 1750 Diderot and his collaborator, Jean d'Alembert, published the prospectus for this multi-volumed project, destined to become one of the great literary monuments of the Enlightenment. The prospectus attracted more than 2,000 subscribers. The aim was to establish an authoritative 'treasurehouse' of all human knowledge, to set out in secular terms the achievements and glories of man's past, and to chart the course of man's future progress. More than 1,000 entries, the work of numerous contributors, cover a wide range of subjects, including religion, philosophy, literature, morality, politics, economics, medicine, history, law, architecture, meta-

alists celebrated it as the origin of all things which, therefore, made the constructions of theology wholly unnecessary. Optimists and pessimists among the philosophes debated just how ready nature was to be dominated, how shrewd or vicious in its resistance, but they agreed that whether man's relation to nature must be viewed as a collaboration or as a duel, that relation was intimate, inescapable, and exclusive. And some philosophes, [Denis] Diderot being prominent among them, saw nature as a refuge from science.

---

physics, mathematics, science, as well as the 'mechanical arts', trades, artisan crafts, industrial and agricultural processes.

The enterprise was weighed down by controversy from the start when in 1752 the abbé [priest, Jean-Martin de] Prades, one of Diderot's contributors, and author of the controversial entry, 'Certainty', was accused of heresy, and distribution of the first two volumes of the *Encyclopedia* was banned. The deep hostility of the clergy was deflected by the protection of [Antoinette Poisson,] Mme de Pompadour and [Chrétien] Malesherbes (the minister responsible for censorship), and publication of the first eight volumes continued undeterred until 1758 when the privilege to print and sell the *Encyclopedia* was again withdrawn. Work had to continue in secret in a climate of increasing hostility from both Church and Government, inflamed in 1757 with the attempted assassination of Louis XV by Robert Damiens, an event for which the encyclopedists were held morally responsible. Opposition intensified still further in 1758 with the publication of [Claude-Adrien] Helvétius' controversial work, *Of the mind*, and again in 1759 with the appearance of d'Alembert's entry, 'Geneva'. Publication proceeded, however, and by 1772 seventeen volumes of double-columned text, together with eleven volumes of superbly engraved plates, had been printed. Seven additional volumes, in which Diderot played no editorial role, appeared between 1776 and 1780.

David Williams, *Denis Diderot: Biographical Note*, in *The Enlightenment*, ed. David Williams. Cambridge, UK: Cambridge University Press, 1999, pp. 291–92.

The result was a curious set of contradictory attitudes toward science that troubled the philosophes' clarity of thought and mitigated their pleasure in the process of scientific investigation. Having made man master in his own house, some of the philosophes felt like strangers in it, and they could not quite suppress their longing for ancient simplicities. This nostalgia was by no means universal among them; on the whole one can say that the philosophes who knew science best feared it least. . . .

Purpose in Nature

Diderot was in a rather more compromising position. He was reluctant to accept the cruel verdict of Newtonian science; he refused to believe in a nature largely empty, populated by cold, colorless corpuscles [cells], and wholly indifferent to moral questions. "Man," Diderot exclaims in an impassioned plea . . . "is the single place from which we must begin and to which we must refer everything"; remove "my existence and the happiness of my fellowmen, and what do I care about the rest of nature?" Man is, and must be, at the center of all things: "If we banish man, the thinking or contemplating being, from the face of the earth, this moving and sublime spectacle of nature will be nothing more than a sad and mute scene. The universe will cease to speak; silence and night will seize it. Everything will be changed into a vast solitude where unobserved phenomena take place obscurely, unobserved. It is the presence of man which makes the existence of beings meaningful." All philosophes agreed that man is important; in fact, they insisted on it. Hume and [Jean Le Rond] d'Alembert, cool precursors of modern scientific objectivity, were wryly willing to concede that man is indeed nature's masterpiece. But Diderot wanted more than that: he wanted man to merge into nature, and draw from it answers to his most pressing questions—What must I do? and, even more significant, Who am I? Diderot found it impossible to live with the teaching, implied by Newton and elaborated by eighteenth-century scientists, that science discloses what is and says nothing about what should be, that truth and beauty, truth and goodness, are wholly distinct.

Nature, [Diderot] insisted . . . is one vast interconnected organic whole in which the steps from matter to life, from science to ethics, from observation to admiration are not merely possible but proper and indeed essential. And so Diderot, looking . . . ahead to the *Naturphilosophie* of the German Romantics, united what scientific philosophy was separating and asked of it what it could not give. "The distinction between a physical and a moral world," he wrote about . . . himself, "seemed to him empty of meaning."

Unprecedented Advances in Knowledge

For all these alarms and evasions, the drift of scientific philosophy toward moral neutrality created some anxiety among the philosophes but no panic; Diderot's distrust of mathematics remained a relatively temperate minority report from the camp of progress.

Science failed to take the monstrous spectral shape it has taken since because, first of all, the really destructive possibilities of technology were still far in the future and almost beyond the imaginative reach of reasonable men. What is more, the philosophes—*all* philosophes—had an enormous investment in science as an ally in their war against religion; it was a commonplace among them that when science advances, superstition retreats. But beyond this, the philosophes found science genuinely admirable for its own sake. It was, with its unprecedented method, vastly superior to the alternative ways of seeking knowledge—the methods of theology and of metaphysics—that men had devised before. Not all new discoveries, especially in the biological sciences, stood above controversy. But that did not matter. They were subject to rules that permitted the testing of proposals, the confirmation and refinement of theories; scientific progress silenced disputes. Decade by decade, sometimes it seemed year by year, the area of agreement grew larger.

Educated men who had grown up amidst the clamor of philosophers and theologians found this astounding. The history of thought, as they well knew, was a history of discord, of endless, fruitless wrangles among the doctrinaire representatives of schools and sects, all claiming possession of infallible truth and denouncing their adversaries as fools or agents of the devil. Skeptics in ancient Alexandria had offered these point-less disputes as advertisements for their own school, which taught a courageous suspension of judgment. Some centuries later, Christian theologians in turn had exploited the quarrels of philosophical sects, and asked men to give up the vain games of reason and embrace the certainties of Christ. But, as the history of dogma proved over and over again, the theolo-gians had been no better than the heathen philosophers: dis-pute and mutual abomination was everywhere, progress and certainty in knowledge nowhere. And now the sciences of na-ture promised a way to knowledge, and an accumulation of knowledge, to which all reasonable men could assent.

This is why the scientific method struck the eighteenth century as an invention unprecedented in its sheer magnifi-cent effectiveness. In this new atmosphere, Voltaire sug-gested, the survival of the epithets "Newtonian" or "Carte-sian" was misleading; scientific groupings were not contesting parties of hate-filled theologians: "What do names matter? What do the places matter where the truths were discovered? We are concerned with experiments and calculations, not with party chieftains."

Science Applied to Man and Society

The momentous manifestation of the scientific method— one of the most significant, most heartening realities in the world of the Enlightenment—promised a momentous con-sequence. If the scientific method was the sole reliable method for gaining knowledge in a wide variety of contexts, from the phenomena of the heavens to the phenomena of plant life, it seemed plausible and in fact likely that it could be profitably exported to other areas of intense human con-cern where knowledge was as primitive now, and disagree-ment as vehement, as it had been in physics a century be-fore—the study of man and society. Even if facts and values were distinct, even if science was not the source of all past values, a bridge could be built between facts and values and the scientific method might become the instrument for the creation of future values. . . .

Significantly enough, it was David Hume, the very philosopher who had insisted on the strictest possible separation of facts and values, who also insisted on the social relevance of scientific enquiry. It is well known that Hume advertised his *Treatise of Human Nature* to be "An Attempt to introduce the experimental Method of Reasoning into Moral Subjects," and his Introduction to the *Treatise* is a manifesto of the Enlightenment's critical positivism, a call to have objective knowledge serve human ends. "'Tis evident," Hume argues, "that all the sciences have a relation, greater or less, to human nature; and that however wide any of them may seem to run from it, they still return back by one passage or another." After all, even *"Mathematics, Natural Philosophy, and Natural Religion"* are to some degree "dependent on the science of MAN"; they "lie under the cognizance of men, and are judged of by their powers and faculties." If this holds for these abstruse disciplines, how much more must it hold for the "other sciences," like logic, ethics, aesthetics, and politics, "whose connexion with human nature is more close and intimate"? Human nature is the capital or center of the philosophical sciences, which "being once masters of, we may every where else hope for an easy victory. From this station we may extend our conquests over all those sciences, which more intimately concern human life." Hume conceded that the establishment of a reliable science of man was a difficult task; it depended on the accumulation of "experience and observation," and, unlike the natural sciences, the science of man could not artificially multiply its observations through experiment. . . . The modern philosopher had every right to be confident: "Where experiments . . . are judiciously collected and compared, we may hope to establish on them a science, which will not be inferior in certainty, and will be much superior in utility to any other of human comprehension." Even if he did not always say what he meant, Hume always meant what he said: the science of man was possible and would be immensely useful. That is why the men of the Enlightenment were ultimately not afraid of science; it was not merely their best, but their only, hope for the knowledge that would give man both abundance and freedom. More than a century before [Sigmund] Freud—the greatest scientist of man the world has known and the philosophes' most distinguished disciple in our century—the philosophes believed, as he would put it later: "No, science is no illusion. But it would be an illusion to suppose that we could get anywhere else what it cannot give us."

Chapter 4

Social History and Culture in Eighteenth-Century Europe

Turning | Points
IN WORLD HISTORY

Economic Expansion and Progress

Leonard Krieger

The social and economic conditions of eighteenth-century Europe are analyzed by Leonard Krieger, professor of history at Columbia University and author of numerous works on political theory. The following article is taken from his book, *Kings and Philosopher: 1689–1789.*

Enlightenment Europe in the eighteenth century entered an era of transition and transformation even though the continent was predominantly conservative, intent on preserving tradition. The *philosophes* and their supporters, who espoused progressive, even radical ideas, actually constituted a small minority of the population. Thus they frequently encountered opposition to the political and religious reforms that they advocated. However, by the end of the century, their ideas prevailed.

In the second half of the eighteenth century the process of change was accelerated by several economic and demographic factors (the latter concerns statistics and data about the population). The population explosion led to rapid urbanization, increased demand for goods, an enlarged labor supply, and industrial growth. Greater prosperity led in turn to the emergence of the educated and middle classes that, together with landowners, were vociferous in their demands for political rights. Finally, the expansion of international trade, particularly in Britain and France and their colonies, not only provided raw materials and created new markets but also facilitated the dissemination of liberal ideas. This surge of economic activity encouraged a flowering of inventive genius, led to progress, and prepared the ground for the Industrial Revolution of the nineteenth century.

Leonard Krieger, *Kings and Philosophers, 1689–1789.* London, UK: Weidenfeld and Nicolson, 1971. Copyright © 1970 by Leonard Krieger. Reproduced by permission of the Literary Estate of Leonard Krieger.

No economic revolution preceded the political revolution that ended the eighteenth century. During the entirety of the period with which we are concerned—that is, until 1789—by far the greater part of the European population lived, and saw no option but to live, in the same kind of corporately organized, hierarchical society that they and their forebears had inhabited since the reestablishment of religious and civil peace in the seventeenth century; and for the vast majority of men this pattern of stability held for all regions from the Urals [in Russia] to County Kerry [in Ireland]. Throughout Europe, in progressive Great Britain as well as in retrograde Russia, most men were still undertaking the significant activities of their lives as members of time-honored associations which channeled these activities along the lines of well-tried custom and imbued these men with the values of the security that is attached to familiar routine. The model existence for which men strove was still to have a rich variety of protective institutions—ideally, a separate institution for each function of life. However distinct from one another in function or membership these institutions were supposed to be—like the organs of the human body to which they were still so often compared—they shared important qualities: they were bound by tradition; they were addicted to ritual; they were organized on the basis of privilege both in their internal structure and in their external relations with one another. For the guarantee of their rights in law and social custom (including the rights to political representation, where such rights were recognized), men were still grouped in a hierarchy of "ranks," "orders," or "estates," as they were variously called. For the pursuit of their occupations they were still subject in varying measure to the regulations of guilds, manors, or peasant communes. For the guidance of personal and social life, local corporations retained a far-reaching autonomy, and they continued to sanction the rules that were administered by local authorities who were powerful precisely because of the corporate tradition they administered: oligarchs were the heads of municipalities, gentry of counties, lords of villages, and in their exercise of controls they were joined by the bishops and local clergy of the established churches, who still registered the great events of personal life, sponsored the social entertainments, and articulated the public conscience.

Growing Tensions

The reality, undoubtedly, was not nearly so harmonious or stable as this model. In the first place, the neat allocation of separate corporations to separate groups and functions had never worked without friction in practice, and particularly in the second half of the eighteenth century the overlap and the competition between different corporations pursuing the same function, between complementary corporations pursuing presumably complementary functions, and between different groups in the same corporation, were exacerbated. Thus the merchants of the burgher estate and the progressive

Eighteenth-Century Social Classes

Eighteenth-century Europe was predominantly an agricultural society dominated by a small but powerful aristocratic class. In western Europe, particularly England and France, where an educated middle class was becoming prosperous and influential, Enlightenment ideas were widely disseminated. The significance of the various social classes is discussed in the following excerpt.

Eighteenth-century society was still overwhelmingly agricultural, despite the growth of cities and the development of an urban middle class in western Europe. On the eve of the Revolution in France, the land of the Enlightenment *par excellence*, some twenty-two million out of a population of about twenty-six million were peasants. In central and eastern Europe the peasantry accounted for an even higher proportion of the population, towns were very small, and the only middle class of any importance was bureaucratic rather than mercantile. Only in Holland (properly called 'The United Provinces') had specific historical and geographical circumstances produced a mercantile society.

In the agrarian societies the dominant group was still the no-

landowners of the noble estate fought over wholesale trade and rural manufacturing. The lay aristocracy came increasingly to dispute the local influence of the clerical aristocracy, in a campaign favored by the growing toleration, in fact more often than in law, of dissenting churches and by the ensuing competition between ecclesiastical establishment and dissent. And within the churches, the gulf between higher and lower clergy grew apace.

But there was also a second disturbance of corporate tradition. Distant authorities, as we have seen, had been encroaching for centuries on the judicial, financial, economic, and ecclesiastical autonomy of the local corporations, and this tendency continued throughout the eighteenth century. Responding in part to the supralocal administrative activities of the ever more numerous officials working and traveling for

---

bility. Nobles enjoyed great privileges, including tax exemptions and rights to payments and services from the peasantry; again, these tended to be very much greater in central and eastern Europe. They had a monopoly of the great offices of Church and state, even where (as in France) they wielded little collective political power.

There were wide differences in wealth and even status between nobles, since in most of Europe nobility was a matter of status—inherited by every child of a noble—rather than possessions; with the result that many were no more than small farmers, and a few were paupers. But when all the differences are allowed for, the aristocratic character of eighteenth-century Europe is undeniable.

The mercantile middle class was becoming increasingly prosperous and powerful in western Europe, particularly in England and France; and it is doubtless significant that it was in these countries, with a relatively large number of educated men and a rapid growth of literacy, that the Enlightenment was brought to birth and widely diffused.

Esmond Wright, ed., *The Expanding World*, rev. ed. London: Hamlyn, 1979, p. 149.

the central agencies, and in part to the extra-corporate economic activities of merchants and factors who ignored guilds to set up their branches or their domestic industries among the rural cottagers, increasing numbers of people were escaping the traditional corporate institutions.

An Era of Change

It is indeed the series of changes in the wonted way of doing and looking at things that makes up the history of the second half of the eighteenth century and that will be our chief concern, but these changes can only be understood if we keep always in mind the integrated structure and the static ideal of the society which contained the activities and retained the allegiance of most Europeans until the end of the Old Regime. This image of a corporately organized and traditionally motivated European people is obviously important both as the constant backdrop against which all changes must be measured and as a reminder not only that the agents of change were a minority, as agents of change usually are, but that in this case they were a minority who did not, until the explosion which ended the Old Regime toward the close of the eighteenth century, succeed in altering the fundamental rules by which men actually lived.

There are, however, two other reasons that are perhaps not so obvious but that also make the remembrance of what did not change in the eighteenth century important for the explanation of what did. First, the active minority that spread the seeds of change, whether in the policy of governments, in the pattern of trade, or in the realm of ideas, did what they did and thought what they thought in full consciousness of the predominantly static society upon which they were operating, and neither their deeds nor their theories are comprehensible without awareness of this valid consciousness of theirs. Second, the persistent commitment of most Europeans to their wonted ways and their familiar values meant that, in response to the dislocations engendered in these ways and values of life by the proponents of change, the conservative leaders were themselves galvanized into action to defend the social establishment. The actual course of change in the later eighteenth century makes sense only in light of the knowledge that it was powered not only by those who wanted change but also by those who unwittingly and unwillingly contributed to the process of change through the novel means they chose to fight it.

For a portrayal of Europe in the second half of the eighteenth century, then, let us turn first to the economic and social relationships which show the factors of stability and mobility in their due proportions.

Effects of Population Growth

The eighteenth century witnessed the takeoff of the population explosion that has continued to our day, surging powerfully against all social barriers in its path. Although the absolute numbers may be unimpressive by our standards, the proportional increase during this initial stage was great enough to overflow the dikes that had been constructed for a less densely packed humanity. Population figures for the eighteenth century are as unreliable as their explanation is uncertain, but their basic tendency seems clear enough: the population of Europe increased considerably, and the increase was markedly greater in the second half than in the first half of the century. According to one plausible estimate, the increase for the century totaled about three fifths, from around 120 million to around 190 million, with two thirds of the increase coming after 1750. The cause of the increase is even more uncertain than its extent. Historians now reject the older explanation of this "vital revolution" in terms of a falling death rate attributable to improvements in the practice of medicine and in sanitation, for these improvements were themselves limited in kind and restricted in incidence. The most probable explanation would seem to be a falling death rate explicable by the retreat of the age-old scourges of man—pestilence, devastation, and hunger—because of ecological changes noxious to the plague-bearing rat, the more disciplined conduct and limited depredations of eighteenth-century warfare, and the acceptance of hardy new crops like the potato as staple items of mass consumption. But a case has also been made for a rising birthrate in localities where a traditional tendency toward early and prolific marriages was given an unprecedented boost by the waning of natural calamities in the eighteenth century.

Although the causes of the population rise may still be debated, there can be little doubt that its effects were far-reaching. Population pressures increased the demand for goods and thereby initiated the chain reaction which stimulated trade and expanded the capitalization of both agriculture and industry. The expansion of the labor supply, especially in such favored areas as Britain and the Low Countries, led to the development of intensive agriculture and of urban labor reservoirs for industrial growth. But in less favored areas, the increase in population resulted in rural overpopulation that forced the subdivision of small farms to the point of agrarian crisis, and created an oversupply of wandering artisans who became tinder for popular uprisings in town and countryside alike. But however diversified its precise economic effects, the constant growth in the numbers and the density of Europe's inhabitants during the eighteenth century had a uniform social effect: whether it pushed people from the family farms into the labor pools of the countryside, from the countryside into the cities, or from the home country into the colonies, everywhere it upset established customs and began to orient men toward change rather than stability as the dominant way of life.

Expansion of International Trade

International trade, for some five hundred years one characteristic activity among many in the undulating kaleidoscope of European life, broke from its duly assigned mooring to become a second major force for economic change. Not, of course, that its incidence was evenly distributed. The growth of international commerce in the eighteenth century occurred mainly in overseas trade, with direct effects upon the great maritime and colonial nations, Great Britain and France, and with diminishing but perceptible effluence, mediated largely through these nations, into the rest of Europe. Although the statistics for trade are almost as inadequate as they are for other eighteenth-century economic activities, some notion of the orders of magnitude involved may be gleaned from such estimates as the fourfold increase in French overseas trade and the fivefold increase in the carrying capacity of the British merchant fleet during the course of the century.

The importance of international trade in European life is evident not only in the rise of the British-French commercial rivalry to the status of the single most important issue in international politics but perhaps even more clearly in the great leap which both of these powers took over such former maritime and colonial competitors as the Netherlands and Spain. For both declining powers, the relative insulation of their international economies from their domestic economies now became a comparative disadvantage. The Netherlands did continue to play an important role in European overseas and transit trade, and Spain retained its colonial system, but for both powers the stagnation of their development in relation to their own past and the decline of their competitive position in relation to their chief rivals testified to the changed role of international trade. Amsterdam, indeed, remained the center of international finance and the Netherlands the chief source of the world's capital during the eighteenth century, but since the Dutch tended increasingly to invest in the more vital economies of other countries, they themselves contributed an international movement of capital to the process of economic development in the industrialized nations. The expanding orbit of international trade came to include Scandinavians, Prussians, Russians, and other new or rejuvenated actors on the maritime mercantile scene. Their entry increased the competition in international commerce, but the economic effect which world trade had on them was limited and the social effect correspondingly different from that in the more mobilized societies of the west.

Great Britain and France, on the other hand, shared a distinctive combination of economic traits: both had a colonial basis for their foreign trade, and both felt the domestic effect of this commerce. But the precise pattern of the trade and consequently of its effects differed for the two countries. By 1789 not only was more than half of the British trade with areas outside of Europe, in comparison with France's one third, but the character of the commerce itself varied. British commerce consisted in general of the importation of raw materials in exchange for manufactured products, as indicated by the intensity of its trade flow with the North American colonies, a relatively prosperous market for manufactures, and with the Baltic region, a source of grain and naval stores. French trade involved mainly the transshipment of foreign raw materials and the export of French natural products—especially wine and spirits—accompanied by only a modicum of cloth manufactures, as was attested by the large role played in French commerce by Spain, Italy, and the Levant—areas with their own handicraft industries and a low effective demand for industrial imports. For the British, consequently, overseas trade contributed substantially to the demand for increased production and for materials to be used in production. By the last third of the century these demands were preparing the change of economic system we know as the Industrial Revolution. In France ever-expanding sectors of the society—aristocrats, peasants, merchants, bankers, and the professional classes—were caught up in the movement and dislocations of a commercialized economy, but without the alterations in economic organization needed to resolve the resulting tensions and insecurity.

Without the direct stimuli of colonies and overseas trade in massive proportions, the other large European nations fell behind Britain and France both in the affluence and in the mobility of their societies. Still, even the less advanced countries experienced the indirect effects of a modest commercial growth stimulated by the oceanic powers, which in conjunction with the direct effects of a population increase and the international political ambitions of the ruling classes, did have consequences for the mainland societies. Essentially, these consequences were of two kinds: first, influential, albeit small and isolated, groups of merchants and landowners were absorbed into the larger network of interlocal exchange; and second, the rulers of these countries adopted economic and social policies geared to the growing material bases of power in the leading mercantile states.

Both these kinds of continental economic development were visible in the pattern of urban growth, for the cities in the underdeveloped sectors of Europe that rose to international prominence in the eighteenth century were themselves of two types, corresponding to the two channels of economic stimulation. First, there were cities like Hamburg, Frankfurt, and Geneva, which through their position on the sea or on the great rivers became transit centers for the exchange of Dutch, British, and French goods and money for inland products. Second, there were the expanding cities of Vienna and Berlin, both of which increased in population to well over 100,000 in response to the demands of the royal court, the administration, and the military for the most modern goods and services. Small wonder that the cities of Europe, capital and provincial, became centers of prosperity, culture, and power that exceeded even the great urban concentrations of the Italian Renaissance.

Groundwork of the Industrial Revolution

The spurs from a growing population and a ballooning overseas trade combined to shake unprecedented numbers of Europeans out of their wonted routine and into the kaleidoscopic world of the distant marketplace. To assay what this change meant for the way in which such men earned their livelihood, let us make clear first what it did not mean. There was no "Industrial Revolution," in the proper sense of the term, during the eighteenth century. The Industrial Revolution refers to the rapid series of economic and social events that enthroned mechanized production as the determining factor in the material life of Western society. This drastic shift of economic control from the directors of natural and manual power to the managers of invested capital would, when it came, involve both the change from machines as isolated, *ad hoc* laborsaving devices to mechanization as a general process transferable to all branches of the economy, and the initiation of a self-sustaining chain reaction through which the comparative advantages of machines would continuously create the industrial and urban social conditions and attitudes favorable to their own extension. The eighteenth century witnessed only the first of these two steps, and it witnessed this introductory phase, moreover, only in Great Britain. Not even in Britain did the second step occur, which would turn technological change into a permanent economic and social revolution. The Industrial Revolution, in short, was a product of eighteenth-century economic and social conditions, but the mechanization they sponsored did not react back upon the economy and society to consummate the revolution until well into the next century.

Because the conditions for the Industrial Revolution first appeared in late-eighteenth-century Britain, this island kingdom may be seen as the most advanced, and therefore the clearest, representative of the commercial system that still dominated the economic development of all Europe. For the inventions that initiated the economic transformation to the industrial era were British not because only the British were inventing or because invention was a different kind of activity in eighteenth-century Britain than it was in Europe then or had been in Britain before—it remained a product rather of practical craftsmanship than of theoretical science—but because Britain experienced in greater degree the factors of economic mobility that were affecting Europe as a whole, and responded in ways that became different in kind. Thus the British inventions of the latter eighteenth century were economically distinctive because here the commercial pressures for increased supplies were so pervasive and the relaxation of social and political bonds was so general that the inventions dovetailed in an economic series altering whole processes of production.

The most obvious factor making for the comparative advantage of the British was their leadership over the rest of Europe in the rate of population growth and in the expansion of international trade—elements directly relevant to the expanded market for textiles which was the primary stimulus for technological innovation. The apparently insatiable demand for cloth led to a contagious imbalance which stimulated inventions all along the production line.

Separate but Not Equal: Rousseau on Women

Diana H. Coole

Diana H. Coole, lecturer in politics at the University of Leeds, has written articles on political theory for leading academic journals. In her book, *Women in Political Theory: From Ancient Misogyny to Contemporary Feminism*, she combines an insightful study of major political thinkers with a well-documented feminist perspective in order to trace the development of misogyny—hatred of women—through the ages. She thus focuses attention on an aspect of political history that is often overlooked or neglected.

In the following excerpt from her book, Coole deconstructs the assumptions about women expressed by Jean-Jacques Rousseau (1712–1778) in his various political and philosophical writings about the origins and nature of human society. Coole analyzes Rousseau's definition of the proper role women should play in his ideal society; she also explains why he would deny to women full rights as citizens and deprive them of any participation in public life. Despite Rousseau's major contribution to Enlightenment thought as one of the most important and influential of the French *philosophes*, his attitude to women is shown by Coole to be condescending. By relegating women to the home in his avowedly paternalistic society, he disparages what he regards as women's distinctive qualities—their "feelings"—even as he professes to praise these qualities.

In his *Discourse on Political Economy*, [Jean-Jacques] Rousseau actually explained why he believed that men *ought* to rule families. 'In the family', he writes, 'it is clear, for several reasons which lie in its very nature, that the father ought to command'. In offering his reasons, Rousseau accepts claims by [Thomas] Hobbes and [John] Locke that authority in the family is indivisible. The case of making the father its repository relies on a variation of Locke's 'abler and stronger' theme, which is now more specifically tied to woman's reproductive function: 'however lightly we may regard the disadvantages peculiar to women, yet, as they necessarily occasion intervals of inaction, this is a sufficient reason for excluding them from this extreme authority'. . . .

The evolution of patriarchal families is associated with other simultaneous developments. It is only with stable couplings that men become aware of their paternity: a knowledge which soon seeks guarantees and justifies control over every aspect of women's lives. It is perhaps no accident that Rousseau sees patriarchy and property emerging simultaneously, even if he does not yet make explicit the causal links between inheritance, private property and legitimacy. . . . [There is] a further significant coincidence: woman's economic dependence on man is introduced simultaneously with his sexual dependence on a *particular* woman, the implication being that women must be made dependent in this manner in order that equal power be sustained between the sexes. Finally, it is germane to note that all these developments coincide with the appearance of language, such that meaning is refined within a specifically patriarchal world. Thenceforth two quite different spheres, each with its own values and significance, will develop: the private, familial one where love, romance and womanhood flourish, and its public antithesis where only men are active. . . .

The Role of Woman

The account of woman and of the education most appropriate to her, occurs primarily in Chapter 5 of *Emile*, although Rousseau illustrates his ideas further in the novel *Julie ou La Nouvelle Héloise*. 'But for her sex', he declares in the former work, 'a woman is a man', she has the same organs and faculties as his male norm. However, her sexual function is soon discovered to suffuse a woman's entire existence; it, rather than her humanity, defines her. For while the 'male is only a male now and again, the female is always a female, or at least all her youth; everything reminds her of her sex; the performance of her function requires a special constitution'. Pregnancy, nursing, childbearing, gaining the father's love and credulity sufficiently to integrate him into the family, all conspire to fill her life.

From the sexual act itself, Rousseau concludes that men are strong and active, evincing power and will, while women are weak and passive, lacking resistance. The argument is reminiscent of Aristotle's except that in the eighteenth century it is no longer feasible to support it with his account of generation (although there are in *Emile* post-natal echoes of the Aristotelian belief that the mother nourishes while the father imparts reason: the 'real nurse is the mother and the real teacher is the father'). Nevertheless, Rousseau goes on to make the same sort of teleological [end-result] deductions, documenting the type of qualities a woman must have in order to fulfil her natural function with virtuosity. Made for man's delight, she must service and charm him since to bear him legitimate children and win his love for them is her proper business. Her duties are to please, attract, counsel and console her mate; to 'make his life pleasant and happy'. In order to cultivate the good reputation that is necessary to persuade her master of her fidelity, she is modest, retiring and devoted. In order to compensate for the man's greater strength she cultivates her own powers, which lie in cunning, beauty, wit and wiles. She rules by gentleness, kindness and tact; by caresses and tears; by modesty, distance and chastity. She simultaneously allures and repels, stimulates her husband's desire only to succumb with reluctance. Although all these qualities require careful nurturing, Rousseau is adamant that they are quite natural. . . .

From the role he ascribes to woman, Rousseau deduces a whole range of 'natural' qualities, from the little girl's preference for dolls as play things to feminine tastes which evince a preference for milk and sweets. All reflect the virtue which is appropriate to the domestic sphere. Woman's right is not to be free and equal but to win love and respect through obedience and fidelity. She has rights only so that she might perform her duties better. . . .

Why Women Should Not Be Citizens

[Susan Moller] Okin [feminist scholar] argues that Rousseau's views on women 'violate all the major principles of his ethics and social theory'. Examples of such violation abound. Rousseau demands equality and autonomy among male citizens but authority and heteronomy in the family. He sees that men cannot be free while they depend on the economic or arbitrary power of other men yet he deliberately fosters women's dependence on husbands, from provision of their daily bread to choice of their religion and judgement of their virtue. He looks back to the originally free and self-sufficient natural man whose liberty is to be recaptured in civil life, yet the natural woman he idealizes is the dependent being of the patriarchal family. He advises male citizens to suppress their private interests on behalf of the General Will, yet he would imprison women in the particularity of domestic life. He sees in men a limitless drive to self-improvement through development of their rational capacities, yet defines women according to natural functions which yield them moral and psychological qualities of a fixed and limited type. In short, if Rousseau's political thinking is inspired by Locke, his sexual beliefs are closer to Aristotle.

The characteristics ascribed to women rob them of the credentials for citizenship: they lack the right sort of reason, autonomy, judgement, sense of justice and ability to consent. We have already seen that Locke probably doubted women's rational qualifications for active political membership but that this only resulted from a lack of opportunity to develop their faculties. Rousseau returns to more traditional claims regarding innate sexual differences here. Although women do have reason, he writes in *Emile*, it is of a practical nature. Woman lacks the accuracy or attention for success in the sciences; she cannot appreciate genius. For abstract and speculative truths, principles and axioms, generalizations as such, are beyond her grasp. Of course, the education that Rousseau advises makes this a self-fulfilling prognosis, but it is of obvious significance in the political sphere where it is just that reasoning of which he finds women incapable, which is required to discern the General Will.

In order for the General Will to emerge, individuals must not only reason but they must do so independently. Should their thoughts be too influenced by others' beliefs or interests, then the delicate balancing of individual differences will degenerate into clusters of particularity. Yet it is impossible to imagine Rousseau's women making any impartial assessment of the public good, since they have been raised to make no independent judgement: their guide is always the question 'what will others think of me?' Appearance is for them everything. They lack a capacity to penetrate to, or articulate, truth. In any case, confinement in the home surely denies to Sophy [in *Emile*] and her sisters the breadth of vision which they need to evaluate public issues. The 'genuine mother of a family', Rousseau insists, 'is no woman of the world, she is almost as much of a recluse as the nun in her convent'. She has her sights fixed on the well-being of her particular family, not on the world outside. She is not therefore predisposed to considerations of impersonal justice and Rousseau goes so far as to suggest that this is a natural limitation: 'woman is made to submit to man and to endure even injustice at his hands'. . . .

Thanks to all these lacunae in their reason, autonomy, judgement and consent, women are thus as unsuited to the ideals of citizenship as are the unreconstructed males of the *Second Discourse*. The only difference is that their shortcomings are natural and hence immutable. It might be argued, of course, that it is in their very feminine qualities (whether natural or acquired) that women are uniquely well-equipped for the sort of communitarian politics Rousseau envisaged. Separated from property acquisition, they are rarely avaricious and inspired by self-gain; associated with infantile and virile dependants, they are well-practised in putting the needs of others before their own; lacking strength, they are used to extending persuasion rather than force. And it is indeed because he recognizes such virtues that Rousseau does ultimately find women indispensable to the just state. But the role they yield remains for him indirect and largely implicit. . . .

The Ideal Balance Between the Sexes

Rousseau's solution [to the problem of conflicting gender roles], however, is to fuse members of the two sexes in a marital unity such that the different qualities can again complement and bind one another; they become virtually one person. Thus he describes the woman as the eye and the man the hand; they 'are so dependent on one another that the man teaches the woman what to see while she teaches him what to do'. There is nevertheless a constant danger that one sex will imitate the other and then the balance will be destroyed. This is why Rousseau counsels sexual segregation outside the home, fearing both men who become effeminate when they are consumed with winning a woman's love and women who compete with men in intellectual endeavours.

Ideally, then, Rousseau believes that mutual dependence will limit the excesses of both sexes. The male uses his strength to rule but also his reason, thereby defusing the particularity to which woman's compassion inclines her. But the woman uses the love which that compassion incites, to temper her husband's competitiveness and coldness, reminding him of the sentimental bonds that unite persons. This is why the female's domestic domain evinces an ethic so different from the public world where 'unbridled passions' of rich and poor have 'suppressed the cries of natural compassion and the still feeble voice of justice, and filled men with avarice, ambition and vice'.

Rousseau's preference for female seclusion in the home is thus twofold. First, it prevents women from taking their particular powers into the public realm, where they would be inappropriate. As he writes in the *Letter to M. D'Alembert*, 'Love is the empire of the fair. Here they must give the law, because in the order of nature, resistance belongs to them, and man cannot surmount this resistance, but at the expense of his liberty'. Because women's natural modesty is always better able to control their sexual desire than men's reason can their own, infatuated males are at a woman's mercy. If her powers are unleashed outside of marriage they are destructive because they entice citizens away from the masculine world of generality and abstract reason, infecting it with rampant desires for particular persons and encouraging illicit relationships. But second, women must also be kept out of public in order to safeguard their natural qualities. Those who participate in the public realm of men themselves quickly develop *amour propre* and then not only do they fail in their guardianship of the compassionate side of human nature, but they use their advantages in the sphere of love to dominate men rather than to assuage them. It is because women are associated through their relationship with their young with a natural compassion, that they must be protected by confinement in the domestic world, where they are awarded a crucial role in sustaining the sentiments which are required for civic virtue. Without their compassion, a regenerating social contract would remain inconceivable. This is perhaps why Rousseau places such great store on the strength of the original mother-child bond: 'when mothers deign to nurse their children, then will be a reform in morals; natural feeling will revive in every heart; there will be no lack of citizens for the state; this first step by itself will restore mutual affection'.

To be good citizens, individuals must not only obey the law as a set of formal instructions; they must identify with it because they see in it an expression of the community, of which they are a part. They must therefore empathize with others and it is just this feeling which women teach. Ironically, it is from their mothers that men first learn the sentiments necessary to patriotism, fraternity and discernment of the General Will. Thus Rousseau asks: 'can devotion to the state exist apart from the love of those near and dear to us? Can patriotism thrive except in the soil of that miniature fatherland, the home? Is it not the good son, the good husband, the good father, who makes the good citizen?' As part of a romantic reaction against the Enlightenment, Rousseau believed that sentiment as well as reason must guide justice. Yet we now see that these two attributes tended to be contributed by the different sexes, united through marriage. Without domestic virtue, in short, there could be no civic virtue; the conventional state does ultimately require a foundation in nature and this can only come from the family. . . .

If women were active in the polity, the differentiations without which justice and liberty could not endure for Rousseau, would collapse. Compassion—self-love; particularity—generality; love—law; personal—impersonal; natural—conventional are all for him oppositions which are simultaneously sustained and harmonized only as long as women and men maintain their diffuse identities in an intimate relationship. The moral complicity of the sexes, who together fuse the originally balanced virtues, is embodied in a family-state dyad. This explains why Rousseau, despite his paranoid denunciation of factions in *The Social Contract*, fails to cite the family as one of those manifestations of particularity that would threaten the state. It is indispensable to it.

Rousseau Adopts Classical Greek View of Women

In conclusion, I do not think that Rousseau's enchantment with the Ancients can be overemphasized here. In essence, he adopts Aristotle's view that women should be excluded from citizenship but accepts, with him, that they might provide its preconditions. In propounding a rather Aristotelian notion of civic virtue, he grants to women an indispensable moral and emotional mission. As he says of the Greek use of slaves, there 'are some unhappy circumstances in which we can only keep our liberty at others' expense'. Like his predecessor, Rousseau distinguishes between beneficiaries and others according to their supposedly natural functions, on the basis of which he ascribes to them an appropriate type of reason and virtue. He imputes to women the typically Greek virtues of fidelity and modesty. He recognizes, like Plato, that the virtues of family life are needed in the just state even while they threaten it, but he must eschew the Platonic/Spartan attempt to overcome the sexual division of function and to collapse the family into the state, otherwise the necessary tensions will not be sustained. His preferred solution, to seclude women in the home and to segregate the sexes even there, is rather that of Aristotle and of classical Athens.

Salons, Mobs, and Mistresses: Women in French Political Life

Susan P. Conner

Susan P. Conner, professor of history at Tift College, Georgia, has contributed articles on French history to various academic publications. Her particular interest is a feminist one—namely, the role of women in French history.

In the following essay, Conner analyzes the various kinds of power wielded by women in eighteenth-century France. Among the most influential women of the time were the *salonnières*—upper-class Frenchwomen who presided over social gatherings of the intellectual elite in their grand reception rooms, or salons. These assemblies, known for their wit, brilliant conversations, and debates about controversial contemporary issues also served to disseminate the ideas of the *philosophes*.

Political power of a very different kind was exercized by those lower-class women who participated in riots to protest the famine and poverty prevalent at the time. These riots often led to mob violence, which was one of the factors that helped precipitate the French Revolution.

Finally, the intrigues of the aristocratic mistresses of nobility and royalty at court are described. Vain, ambitious, and treacherous, these women attempted to use their sexuality to achieve power; but by doing so, they ensured that whatever political influence they attained was tenuous and temporary. Condemned by modern feminist scholars, these women are regarded as having debased the role of women at court.

"Politics are like a labyrinth," wrote William Gladstone [British politician]. They lure participants into a maze. They entangle the curious, they ensnarl the unwary, they obsess the ambitious. While Gladstone was writing about nineteenth-century politics, the politics of eighteenth-century France were no different. Strategies, tactics, and struggles for influence were conducted in the serpentine passages and corridors to power.

The eighteenth century, which is generally dated from the death of Louis XIV in 1715, was a period of sporadic international war, political intrigue, religious controversy, and diplomatic revolution. In France, controversies from previous centuries appeared again. . . .

Frenchwomen's Influence on Politics

According to contemporaries, eighteenth-century politics had also fallen under the influence of women. Looking back over the century, portrait painter Mme [Elisabeth] Vigée-Lebrun wrote, "The women reigned then, the Revolution dethroned them." The influence that women exerted, however, did not originate in the law. As [Charles-Louis de Secondat de] Montesquieu observed, women had accumulated power through conspiracy. Such a base of power might be viewed as ephemeral, but to the *philosophe*, women had become "an estate within the state." That was a fact worthy of note to Montesquieu, and his fictional characters in *Lettres persanes* [*Persian Letters*] told his readers about it. "Anyone at the court, in Paris, or in the provinces," said Rica [a Persian traveler in Europe], "who judges the ministers, magistrates, and prelates without knowing the women who govern them is like a man who can easily tell that a machine works, but who has no knowledge of the inner springs.". . .

The Political Action of Women in Riots

Evidence abounds documenting outbreaks of . . . bread riots, and localized challenges to conscription and taxation that were taking place throughout the century. But was this a form of collective political action in which women participated? On this question, scholars disagree radically. To Jeffrey Kaplow [historian], the crowds of pre-Revolutionary Paris were "pre-political." Women, many of whom participated frequently, were drawn into demonstrations because of their economic misfortunes. As wives and mothers who could not feed their families, they demanded that the government intervene to assist them. There was no desire for political change; there was no conscious challenge to the system. The women were instead governed by fears of famine and insecurity that drove them to riot. To Kaplow, no collective action to change the political system occurred until the Revolution took place. Other scholars, however, disagree. Darline Levy and Harriet Applewhite [feminist scholars] suggest that eighteenth-century demonstrations were politically motivated and were directed with "a certain modicum of political skill." Working-class women had discovered that they had the power to threaten the governing authority. Violence, although outside the formal system, could conceivably effect change. . . . The women participants, therefore, could not be "pre-political" beings.

The answer to this question of political action probably lies somewhere in between the two positions. While an undeveloped political consciousness existed, the political organization to carry out change did not. Throughout the century, years of dearth and famine were also years of bread riots, in particular during the years 1725, 1739–1740, 1752, 1768, and . . . 1775; however, the demonstrations made no lasting change, and the institution of the government was not challenged. On that count, George Rudé [social historian] pointed out, "The main lesson of 1775 was, in short, that . . . no isolated movement of wage-earners, artisans and village poor could hope to yield revolutionary results." Yet riots had continued throughout the century, led by people who had no legal rights to participate in the governing process or to challenge it. By the time of the Revolution, a metamorphosis had taken place, and the result was politically explosive. The scarcity of bread was consciously understood to be bound to the institution of the government. From 1789 on, demonstrations were no longer localized, and political as well as economic goals were evident. Popular violence became a "political tool" of the laboring men and women. . . .

Influential Women at the French Court

Although the *salonnières* of eighteenth-century France remained outside the realm of political action and the wage-earning poor women of Paris can at best be described as marginally political, a handful of women did influence the affairs of state and wield political power. These few political personalities were extremely visible in French affairs. They were the women whom Montesquieu and his compatriots believed were dominating politics. "Since Francis I," wrote Melchior Grimm [eighteenth-century cultural historian], echoing Montesquieu's observations, "women have played an important role in the court. In the only country in Europe where custom, not law excludes women from succession to the throne, it is unique that they nevertheless can reign as regents and rule, in fact, as wives and mistresses." Grimm was correct that for several centuries tradition within the elite and royal society had given a few highly placed women an avenue to power. In the sixteenth century, Margaret of Angoulême and Catherine de Medici established a tradition of political involvement followed by Marie de Medici, her favorite Leonora Galigaï, Anne of Austria, and [Françoise d'Aubigné,] Mme de Maintenon in the seventeenth century. From religious disputes to domestic and foreign affairs to women's questions, their influence was present.

Powerful but Treacherous Women at the French Court

During the eighteenth century, the influence of women continued to be an individual effort. These few *femmes de la haute société* [women of the aristocracy], however, were notorious rather than noteworthy for their work, and rather than being models for later feminists, their methods generally have been regarded with scorn. All were born into the nobility, frequented it, or were granted titles. All of them were also influence peddlers, inveterate seductresses, or coquettes, who seemed to represent the abuses of the ancien régime and who had no interest in pursuing social or political changes that would have supported equality between the sexes. All of these women consciously laid plans to increase their power over politics and the men who made decisions concerning affairs of state. Because of the legal exclusion of women from the government, their influence came through informal channels to power. In the pre-Revolutionary eighteenth century, women and politics were synonymous with intrigue.

The Mask of Manners in Civilized Society

Jean Starobinski

The contrast between barbarism and civilization was a controversial topic of discussion by the *philosophes* in the era of the Enlightenment. Jean Starobinski, professor of French literature at the University of Geneva, renowned Enlightenment scholar, and the author of numerous academic works, gives a penetrating analysis of the complexities of this subject. The following essay is excerpted from his book, *Blessings in Disguise; or, The Morality of Evil*, which was awarded two prestigious literary prizes.

Many of the *philosophes* insisted that civilization was a source of moral corruption and not, as was generally assumed, the ideal form of human society. Starobinski proceeds to explain how such an inversion of values occurred. In the early eighteenth century the word *civilization* usually had positive connotations: It was associated with improvement, refinement, culture, comfort, and polite manners. Indeed by the end of the century, civilization was seen to embody the concept of progress. Various inquiries into the stages of such progress led to the conclusion that civilization represented a process of gradual evolution from savagery and barbarism to industrial, commercial society. At the same time, others maintained that civilization was not a process but rather the end product of history, the final condition of mankind at the high point of evolution. Yet whatever assumption was made, whether process or end product, the concept of civilization postulated its

Jean Starobinski, "The Word Civilization," in *Blessings in Disguise; or, the Morality of Evil*, translated by Arthur Goldhammer. Cambridge, MA: Harvard University Press, 1993. Copyright © 1993 by the President and Fellows of Harvard College. Originally published in *Le remède dans le mal: Critique et lègitimation de l'artifice á lâge des Lumières*. Paris: Editions Gallimard, 1989. Copyright © 1989 by Editions Gallimard. Reproduced by permission of Editions Gallimard. In the United States by Harvard University Press.

opposite—a primordial original state, whether of savagery or of some other precivilized condition. The implications and details of this primordial condition aroused much speculative inquiry.

While the *philosophes* were speculating, travelers to the New World returned with enthusiastic descriptions of its indigenous inhabitants. These reports proved to be detrimental to the so-called "civilized" people of Europe. Having observed humankind in what was assumed to be its natural or primordial state, many travelers concluded that it was superior in many respects to civilization. Yet there were still those who persisted in believing that the human primordial state was savage and barbaric. In general, ambivalent attitudes to civilization continued to prevail.

Most of the *philosophes* (especially Jean-Jacques Rousseau) maintained that the politeness and refined manners of so-called "civilized" society merely served to mask its underlying barbarism and corruption. They regarded good manners as deceit and condemned the civilized code of conduct as hypocrisy. These *philosophes* argued that human beings in their primordial state, however crude and savage, were at least open and honest in their behavior.

[Honoré-Gabriel de Riqueti] Mirabeau's abundant writings fail to ascribe a single clear meaning. He implies that because civilization is not a universal or linear process, it constitutes only a brief apogee in the cycle of social existence, in the "*natural circle* from barbary to decadence by way of civilization and wealth." History would thus consist of cycles, and presumably certain nations, having been through all phases of the cycle, had simultaneously achieved a pinnacle of perfection. . . .

Elsewhere, Mirabeau uses the word *civilization* to refer not to a process but to a state of culture and material abundance. "The movable wealth of a nation depends . . . not only on its civilization but also on that of its neighbors."

Thus even in the writings of the first man to use the word, *civilization* was apt to take on plural meanings. When it referred to a process, it was a process that had occurred several times in history only to give way, each time, to ineluctable decadence. When it referred to a more or less stable state, that state was one that might take different forms in different nations. Civilization was not one but many.

Here, of course, ancient history was a tacit source of models. Rome was the great example of an empire that had traversed the "circle of civilization." From Herodotus, from Polybius, Plutarch, Tacitus, and Ammianus Marcellinus [ancient historians], modern writers had learned to compare the Greeks and the Persians, the Greeks and the Romans, the Romans and the barbarians.

From the outset, then, it was clear that the word could take on a pluralist, ethnological, relativistic meaning yet retain certain implications of the most general sort, implications that made "civilization" a unitary imperative and determined the unique direction of "march" of all humankind.

Civilization and Savagery

Before the word *civilization* was coined or disseminated, an extensive critique of luxury, refined manners, hypocritical politeness, and the corruption due to the cultivation of the arts and sciences was already in place. From Montaigne to Rousseau . . . many . . . travelers to the New World, moreover, the comparison of the civilized man with the savage (and even the cannibal) did not favor the former. Accordingly, . . . Mirabeau sought to distinguish true from false civilization in the realm of *fact* as well as *value*. In a manuscript entitled . . . "The Friend of Women, or Treatise on Civilization"; probably from 1768, Mirabeau insisted on the moral criterion that authenticates civilization and without which the whole code of manners and and the sum total of learning are mere masks:

> I am astonished, when it comes to civilization, at how distorted our thinking is. Ask most people what their idea of civilization is and they would answer that it is perfection of manners, urbanity, and politeness and diffusion of knowledge such that the proprieties are observed in the absence of detailed regulations—all of which to me is but the mask of virtue and not its true face, and civilization does nothing for

society if it does not establish the foundations and form of virtue. It is in societies made soft by the aforementioned factors that the corruption of humanity begins.

No sooner was the word *civilization* written down, in other words, than it was found to contain a possible source of misunderstanding. In another text Mirabeau speaks of "false civilization." In still another he goes so far as to obliterate the distinction between barbarian and civilized by denouncing "the barbarity of our *civilizations*." . . . The word no longer refers to a process but to a state—and it is a state that does not deserve its name. The plural implies that each of the nations of contemporary Europe has its own civilization, but that instead of getting rid of the violence of "primitive" societies these civilizations perpetuate the brutality beneath deceptive exteriors. Instead of open barbarity contemporary civilizations practice a dissimulated violence.

Clearly, the word *civilization*, as used by its French "inventor," did not possess a single, unequivocal meaning. The concept was novel in its very form, but it was not initially considered to be incompatible with the traditional spiritual authority (religion). On the contrary, it was a product of that authority. It referred to a process of perfecting social relations and material resources, and as such it stated a "value" and defined what might be called an "ideal." It was coupled with the imperatives of virtue and reason. Yet the same writer also used the term in a purely descriptive and neutral sense to denote the range of institutions and technologies that all the great empires possessed at their peak and lost when they fell into decadence. Societies, it was conceded, could differ in structure without forfeiting the right to be embraced within the general concept of civilization. Finally, the term applied to the contemporary situation with all its irregularities and injustices. Civilization in the latter sense was the object of critical reflection, whereas civilization in the ideal sense described above was a normative concept on the basis of which it was possible to discriminate the civilized from the uncivilized, the barbarian, and the incompletely civilized. The critique thus took two forms: a critique of civilization and a critique formulated in the name of civilization.

Civilization belongs to the family of concepts that either define an opposite or are formulated in order to permit the definition of an opposite. "Greek" and "barbarian" are linked notions. "Without the Greek," François Hartog reminds us, "there is no barbarian." Communities of people who speak the *true* language must exist in order for others to be considered "mute," incapable of speech (which is the root meaning of "barbarian").

Before *rusticus* . . . can be defined as antonym of *urbanus*, . . . there must be cities and people who live in cities. And only a person who lives in a city can boast of superior *civility* or regret, in melodious and exquisitely studied verse, the loss of pastoral happiness or Arcadian tranquillity. . . .

Politeness

[A common] strategy was to take a term like *civility*, initially highly valued but later taken to connote complicity in deception, and introduce alongside it a second term cleansed of all suspicion. The second term then became a substitute for the first, which subsequently lost all value. Thus *politeness*, which was at first virtually a synonym for *civility*, gained preference among lexicographers and moralists until it too became tainted by suspicion.

If civility is simply the external expression or artificial imitation of politeness, politeness can be seen as a deceptive art, a way of imitating absent virtues. It can be attacked in the very same terms as civility. Already at the end of the seventeenth century [Jean de] La Bruyère could write: "Politeness does not always inspire goodness, equity, toleration, gratitude; it gives at least the appearance of those things and makes man appear outwardly as he ought to be inwardly." There is no need to multiply examples. The pattern is always the same: an ostensible virtue is discredited by reducing it to a mere outward appearance, a sham, instead of something truly inherent in an individual, group, or society. Reduced to mere appearances, politeness and civility give free rein, inwardly, in depth, to their opposites, malevolence and wickedness—in short, to violence, which was never truly forsaken. Or so it appears by the light of the critical torch, which has been raised to bare the contradiction between appearance and reality, between the flattering mask and the true face, wherever it can. Accusatory thought finds inauthenticity wherever it looks. Thus in terms of moral substance, rigorous scrutiny generally inverts the meaning of "civilized" and "savage." This reversal is best expressed by [François-Marie Arouet de] Voltaire, who, when his Huron [character in a philosophical tale] is locked up in the Bastille, has him say: "My compatriots in America would never have treated me so barbarously; they cannot even imagine it. People call them savages. They are good people but crude. And the men of this country are refined scoundrels." The adjectives "crude" and "refined," which express the accidental, the apparent, are linked to nouns that capture the—radically different—underlying reality: good people, scoundrels.

Chapter 5

The Legacy of the Enlightenment

Turning | Points
IN WORLD HISTORY

The Feminist Legacy in France

Claire G. Moses

Claire G. Moses, editor of the journal *Feminist Studies* and author of a book on French feminism, teaches women's studies at the University of Maryland. In the following article, she describes the emergence and development of French feminism during the last three centuries.

According to this article, the radical changes in the image and status of women in eighteenth-century France are difficult to evaluate. On one hand, what Moses terms "a collective female consciousness" emerged after the French Revolution. On the other, as she indicates, women were still repressed as the era ended.

By the nineteenth century, the feminist movement had acquired new vigor, in part because attitudes promulgated in the eighteenth century continued to serve as catalysts for change in the nineteenth. During this period, sexual liberation helped shape the feminist agenda, but repressive laws in France still infringed on woman's rights and freedom.

Only in the late nineteenth and early twentieth centuries did women finally acquire the legal and political rights for which they had long fought—including full citizenship and the vote. Moses concludes by arguing that without the demands made by women of independent minds during the Enlightenment, the emancipation of women in France would likely not have been achieved.

In eighteenth-century France, both the image and reality of women were undergoing profound changes. These changes extended forward into the nineteenth and twentieth centuries and explain the modern concept of French womanhood. Our examination of eighteenth-century views on women will conclude by highlighting the connections that link the experience of eighteenth-century French women to French women's future experiences. . . .

The most important of the feminist publicists during the early years of the Revolution were [Marie-Jean de Caritat de] Condorcet, Olympe de Gouges, Etta Palm d'Aelders, and Théroigne de Mericourt. In their writings, the basic concepts of Enlightenment reasoning are made to pertain to women as well as to all men. Their feminism paralleled the Revolution's politics of individual rights. They believed that individuals of both sexes were similar in capacity and character, and they ascribed male-female differences to socialization. Sex, no more so than social position at birth, should not be a cause to deny the basic rights of citizenship. Justice required that all men *and* women be assured the opportunity to develop their full potential.

A phenomenon of nearly equal importance was the development of a collective female consciousness, resulting from women's participation in the Revolution. A few women took part in the disturbances of July 14, 1789, and again of the night of August 4, but they were notable for their singularity. The "October Days" of that same year, however, were a women's affair; and women participated in important numbers in the Champ de Mars demonstration of 1791, as they did again on 4 Prairial (1795). Parisian women participated in politics through the "mixed fraternal societies," which had been created to inform and instruct "passive" citizens—including women—of the actions of the Revolutionary government. In the provinces, clubs of entirely female membership sprang up. Although for the most part, the women in these provincial clubs seemed to have understood their role to be that of auxiliary supporters to the male makers of the Revolution, their activities encouraged the emergence of a sense of the collective power of women.

Male Opposition of Feminism

The opposition likely sensed this nascent [emerging] collective force. By the fall of 1793, all of the feminist activists found themselves at one or another point along the spectrum of the political opposition, and the Committee on General Security moved to silence them. The prosecution quickly widened from an attack on a frankly feminist group, such as the Société des Républicaines Révolutionnaires, to all women who dared to participate in politics. The violent reaction against women's political activities, frequently believed to have been inspired by Napoleon, was, in fact, already in motion by 1793.

Rousseau's Views on Women

This reaction can, of course, be understood simply as a reemergence of a seemingly eternal patriarchal system, but such an explanation would overlook its historically specific characteristics. Jacobin [radical] arguments against women's political activities were not some mere throwback to "unenlightened" times. Rather, Jacobins relied on the quite new reasoning formulated by [Jean-Jacques] Rousseau. As Gita May has made clear, Rousseau was unlike earlier patriarchalists. He depicted a middle-class, not upper-class, existence and specifically a kind of middle-class life that had not existed in earlier centuries when workplace and home overlapped. He glorified the separation of private and public spheres and elevated bourgeois women's newly time-consuming maternal preoccupations to an exalted level. Women's role as men's companion was elevated too; they were indispensable to men's happiness, and, in recognition, Rousseau's men loved and respected them. Women's innate aptitude for love and selfish devotion thus assured them dignity, respect, and happiness. In some ways, Rousseau reads more like women's defenders in the earlier, seventeenth-century *querelle des femmes* [women's quarrel] than their detractors.

But Rousseau's appreciation of women's familial role was central to arguments that actually strengthened older patriarchal values by reformulating them in terms that were relevant to eighteenth-century society. It was women's maternal responsibilities that now required her exclusion from the kind of civil, political, and economic activities that Rousseau championed for all men. Rousseau had changed the patriarchal concept of womanhood from one that was similar in quality but lesser in value to one that was qualitatively different and, if not lesser than, still subordinate to men. . . .

Repression of Women at End of Eighteenth Century

That the eighteenth century ended in repression is, therefore, neither surprising nor even anachronistic. The uniform legal system that rationalist jurists spent more than a decade drawing up enshrined the Rousseauist concept of the difference of women from men. The Civil Code recognized the rights of all citizens but excluded women from the definition of citizenship. Women were thereby reduced to the status of a legal caste at the same time that the ancien régime's legal class system was abolished for men. Women's status worsened—if not in absolute terms, then in relative terms. Indeed, even in absolute terms, *some* women's status worsened, for when many different laws had applied differently to French people from different geographic areas or from different orders there had existed opportunities for women, especially noble women, to escape the full harshness of patriarchal laws. They could slip through loopholes created by differing and overlapping legal systems. Those opportunities had now been erased, and this was the meaning, for women, of the new civil equality.

Eighteenth-century views on women were contradictory, then, providing encouragement for the emergence of a feminist movement but also new weapons to gun it down. On balance, however, the movement was forward because even seemingly patriarchal views, like Rousseau's, contained the seeds of new power for women that bore fruit in the following century.

The View of Women in Nineteenth-Century France

In nineteenth-century France, the romantic woman—a direct descendant of Rousseau's [fictional] Julie—was idealized. This rehabilitation of women in theory was the foundation upon which a feminist movement would be constructed.

Women's self-esteem was elevated by their positive depiction in popular literature. As a result, some were emboldened to question the continuing limitations placed on their activities. Not surprisingly, nineteenth-century feminists were ambivalent about the image of the good, romantic woman. They recognized that this literary personnage was no equal to man; she was child-like, dependent on men's power for her very survival, or self-sacrificing, subordinating herself to men's interests. Nonetheless, feminists frequently employed romantic language idealizing women to further their cause. Its usefulness for feminist purposes was undeniable.

There was a relation, too, between the creation of a legal system based solely on sex and the reemergence of feminism in the nineteenth century. The [Civil] Code served as a rallying point for feminist protest not only because it discriminated against women but also—and perhaps more significantly—because it intensified women's sense of sex identification. By proclaiming the political significance of sex, the Code ironically participated in the shaping of feminist consciousness.

The continuing influence of eighteenth-century thought on women is evident, too, in the subsequent development of the French feminist movement. In nineteenth-century France, the utopian socialists were the first to discuss feminist ideas. During the 1830s and 1840s, their teachings reached an audience throughout the Western world. Feminism moved beyond isolated concern to become an international collective force. . . .

Nineteenth-Century Feminists Proclaim Sexual Liberation

During the 1830s, utopian feminists had also taught that women's liberation and sexual liberation were interconnected issues, but by 1848, they had rejected this notion. Here, too, the shift in feminist theory is explained by changes in women's lives dating to the eighteenth century. Utopian visions had been overwhelmed by the reality of a dramatic increase in the ratio of "illegitimate" births to total births that had begun about mid–eighteenth century. Until 1750, illegitimacy had been essentially unknown in ancien régime France; by the mid–nineteenth century, it accounted for between five and ten percent of all births in France, and in certain areas—especially Paris, Lyons, and Bordeaux—illegitimacy accounted for between thirty and fifty percent of all births.

Feminists—many of whom had attempted to live the new morality of "free love"—came to the sad conclusion that sexual liberation without economic liberation or political rights was a chimera. Large numbers of young women were working in large cities far from their parents. Their geographical mobility had left them bereft of traditional familial support systems. Throughout the century, women on their own—even without a child to support—could not earn wages sufficient to support themselves. Exploitative conditions in the work force carried over to sexual relations. Example after example in literature attested to the exploitative nature of sexual relations outside of marriage, which commonly involved a woman from the lower classes and her employer of the upper classes. Almost half of the illegitimate children born in Paris in the 1880s were born to servant mothers, but employers were protected against their servants' claims by the legal system.

The feminist program after 1848 was shaped by this reality. Feminists demanded a legal solution to the problems raised by illegitimacy and supported changes in the Code that would permit divorce and paternity suits, establish inheritance rights for illegitimate children, and eliminate prostitution. At the same time, they insisted that the most obvious solution to illegitimacy was the best solution: sexual abstinence for the unmarried. Their feminism was based on their arguing that this morality apply to men as well as to women.

Feminist Demands in the Nineteenth Century

They demanded, too, the rights and opportunities for an independent existence. At the head of their platform reappeared the centuries-old demand for improved educational opportunities, which after the establishment of a state system of secondary schools for girls, in 1880, became the specific demand that girls' education be made equal to boys'. Next, feminists demanded the right to work. For bourgeois women, this slogan meant opposition to laws that denied them access to the professions. For working-class women, it meant opposition to the so-called protective laws that limited their earning power and the demand that their wages be raised to the level of mens'.

After the Republic was secured in 1879, feminists were hopeful that their demands would be met. They fashioned a kind of politics that was patterned after that of the Opportunist Republicans, whom they challenged. They reasserted the language of individual rights that stressed the "justice" of their cause and focused on issues that could be resolved by legal reforms. At first, their campaign to change the Civil Code highlighted women's exclusion from the rights of citizenship; they demanded that women be allowed to be witnesses to public acts, notaries, and guardians to children in addition to their own and that women be allowed to control their own earnings and share the father's authority over the children and over the community property as well. But, soon, some feminists were urging that the demand for the vote should be put first in their program; in 1909, the Union Française pour le Suffrage des Femmes united formerly fragmented feminists into one block aimed at enfranchising women.

How well did feminists fare? That their struggle was uphill and their victories slow in coming is not surprising given the strength of the patriarchal legacy of the eighteenth century. Nonetheless, the contradictions of that legacy afforded them opportunities as well. Feminists were most successful when those who controlled power shared the liberal values of the Enlightenment or the radicalism of Revolutionists. Unfortunately, this was only intermittently so in nineteenth-century France. Saint-Simonian activities, encouraged by the upheavals of the Revolution of 1830, were curtailed by the government in 1832 and again in 1834. From 1848 to 1850, the feminists could organize clubs and publish newspapers, but, in 1851, the government cracked down on them. An entire generation of feminist leadership was exiled; most never returned to France. Repressive laws on the press and assembly were not lifted until the final years of the Second Empire; and only then did new leaders recommence the propaganda effort. Then came the repression of the Commune uprising, and the working-class participants of the nascent feminist movement were punished, most of them by exile. The rights to organize, lecture publicly, and publish freely were necessary preconditions for further success. The Enlightenment had legitimized these safeguards in theory; in reality, they were not secured for almost another century.

Feminist Achievements in the Late Nineteenth and Twentieth Centuries

Only in 1879 were the rights of feminists to publish and meet publicly ensured. Their achievements in the decades that followed were significant: 1) 1880: a state system of secondary education for girls; 2) the opening up of the university to women—1866, faculté de médecine; 1870, faculté des lettres, sciences, et droit; 1896, école des beaux-arts; 3) 1884: the reestablishment of divorce; 4) the right to practice certain "public" professions—1881, newspaper publisher; 1885, medicine; 1900, law; 5) 1897: the right to witness public acts (single women only); 6) 1898: the right to vote for judges of the *tribunes* [courts] *de commerce*; 7) 1907: the right to vote for members of the conseils de prud'hommes; 8) 1907: the mother's right to equal authority with father over their children; right of mothers alone, in case of "illegitimate" children, to exercise the "paternal" authority; and right of married women to control their own earnings; 9) 1912: the right to initiate a paternity suit; 10) 1919: the Chamber of Deputies passed a universal suffrage bill; 11) 1924: girls' *lycées* adopted a course of study preparatory for the baccalaureate.

Then the pace of change slowed. The feminist movement proved too weak to withstand the reaction that swept all Western countries, France included, in the period that followed. Most notable was the inaction of the Senate on the suffrage bill. French women had to await the total defeat of the Vichy Right before winning the right to vote. An ordinance of the Provisional Government, dated April 21, 1944, finally recognized their most basic right of citizenship. The eighteenth-century agenda had been fulfilled.

The Seeds of Change Come to Fruition

Because change is continuous and recognizes no special moment at the turn into a new century, characteristics of the lives of French women in the nineteenth century—and even into the twentieth century—are evident already in the eighteenth century. But the historical record for that time was contradictory. The Revolution, for example, had witnessed the first burst of feminist activity, but this turned out to be short-lived. The codification of civil and criminal laws a decade later froze the inferior position of women into French jurisprudence. It is an irony that history's celebration of the remarkable ideals and slogans advanced by the Revolution overlooks the almost total interdiction of civil and political rights for women.

Yet [one can] read the record of this historical period and judge their significance for women positively. Such an interpretation requires a look beyond the eighteenth century and into the future. There, we can see how important these years were for the future development of feminism and for the undermining of eighteenth-century arguments against sexual equality. Whereas, prior to 1789, favor for the ideas of the emancipation of women—or at the least, for greater opportunities for women—was restricted to the upper classes and support was usually in the form of approving women's desire for a better education, a feminism more sweeping in its scope and more inclusive in its following had arisen with the Revolutionary upheavals. Eighteenth-century feminists not only added new demands to their program—the rights of full citizen participation in politics and government, the right to work, the right to equality in marriage, and even the right to share the burdens of a nation at war—but they also adopted new methods to obtain their goals. They comprehended that political action was more than a "demand"; it was a means to achieve their demands. They had grasped the potential strength of collective female action. The eighteenth century had bequeathed to the future the *means* to women's liberation.

The Enduring Spirit of the Enlightenment

Ira O. Wade

Ira O. Wade, John J. Woodhull Professor of Modern Languages, Emeritus, at Princeton University and distinguished scholar, has published extensively on the Enlightenment. The following essay is taken from the conclusion of his two-volume study, *The Structure and Form of the French Enlightenment.*

In his analysis of the ideology of the Enlightenment, Wade attempts to define the spirit of the age. Among the widespread beliefs that he finds characteristic are the following: optimism arising from faith in the possibility of achieving happiness on Earth; a belief in progress combined with the assumption that human society is capable of continued improvement through reform; and a celebration of reason allied to pride in the advances made in the arts, philosophy, and the natural sciences.

In France, people of diverse backgrounds were united by the realization that religion presented a formidable obstacle to human development and progress. Critical of the oppressive power of the church, the *philosophes* and their followers opposed institutionalized religion. According to Wade, the vacuum created by a weakened religion was then filled by secular values—namely humanism and the political struggle for liberty and equality.

Wade sums up what he regards as the most enduring ideas of the Enlightenment. These can be found in the writings of three *philosophes*. François-Marie Arouet de Voltaire (1694–1778) asserted that the enlightened mind enhances humanity's capacity for the making of civilization. Jean-Jacques Rousseau (1712–1778) affirmed the creative ability of the heart. And Denis Diderot (1713–1784) emphasized the power of change. The legacy that the Enlightenment bequeathed to future generations is their combined vision of the world.

The Enlightenment as it developed clearly showed not only the flaws in the Ancien Régime but also the permanent defects in the nature of things. The critical spirit was acutely active in finding defects in every category of life, but the philosophes also often recognized that in many respects much progress was being made. The comment was widespread that in the areas of religion, morality, and politics, much reform was necessary; in the areas of natural science, humanism, and the arts, there was confidence that progress could be noted. However, there seems to have developed a general feeling that a struggle between tradition and modernism was causing misery in all the categories. This battle between respect for the past and a desire for change was also introducing confusion in all the categories, but it was most acutely felt in religion, morality, and, to a lesser extent, in art. It was likewise bothersome in politics and economics, but no longer a serious issue in natural science. The evidence clearly indicates, nevertheless, that the power of ideas, thought, and learning in all its broad aspects was now rightly encyclopedic, propagandistic, and vital to the good life. The fundamental notion which directed the whole movement of Enlightenment was that enlightenment was the indispensable means of assuring that good life. The human mind, enlightened by awareness of the phenomena of the universe, could be trusted to guide the individual man and his society to a richer, more enjoyable future. Happiness was now thought very possible.

Of course, this reason for optimism was countered by a keen awareness of the flaws which still endured, and a good deal of exasperation was expressed at their presence. Moreover, between utopia and the realistic assessment of life, the forces of realism were obviously winning out, but not without some very difficult moments. The sense of human limitations was ever-present, countered by the vague yearning for a world of dreams. There were some real human achievements; tolerance, humanitarianism, political and civil freedom, and a desire for justice were plainly noticeable in the midst of some intolerance, much class hatred, some despotic acts, and injustices. There was a strong feeling on the part of many that reform was the way of the world. Many accepted [François-Marie Arouet de] Voltaire's assessment that man, though capable of continual improvement, is nonetheless limited by his humanity. Just as many felt that [Jean-Jacques] Rousseau's tightly wrought search for identity in a world consciously trying unmercifully to suppress that identity had achieved in all the spheres of human activity new ways to release human forces. Though tightly wrought, Rousseau's approach to the meaning of his world was as rationally fashioned as Voltaire's and far more spiritually expressed. The grave tendency on our part to perceive in Rousseau's thought a new drive toward utopia is undoubtedly a mistake. It is a drive toward self-realization in which the yearning for the ideal fulfills the role of the human mind in Voltaireanism. It is thus fully as rational, but it unveils a new form of idealism which increases existence and elevates idealism to a world of dream far beyond Voltaire's world of common sense, but not necessarily opposed to it. Rousseau, for all his difficulties with [Denis] Diderot, is the connecting link between the prudence of Voltaire and the drive to esthetic self-realization by Diderot.

Religion and Politics

On the other hand, there was a strong and widespread feeling that religion was the common enemy. This belief often turned into a fanaticism against Christianity which was unbelievably strong. [Daniel] Mornet, [Paul] Hazard and, indeed, practically everybody else who studies this moment, note this opposition to religion with some astonishment. It was certainly a genuine opposition. There were many at the time who believed sincerely that it would be possible to replace it with a simple natural law which was looked upon as a natural religion. The feeling was widespread that obedience to God's will, love of one's fellow man, and a charity which expressed itself in human justice were possible without a cult, a formal Church hierarchy, and a complicated greed. I know many who had a deep hatred of Catholicism, chiefly because of the religious persecutions. There were few who really were true atheists in the modern sense of the term. There is some evidence, however, that even the deists and many of the critics of Christianity felt that there was something monolithic in religion which could not be reformed. History after the Revolution proved that such an opinion was premature, but not until much damage had been caused in the area of religion.

It is evident that this opposition to religion had been going on since the beginning of modern times in the very early Renaissance. After the middle of Louis XIV's reign, the movement was accelerated, but after 1750, it was swifter still. Everybody agrees that the big break which occurred was brought about by a savage attack against Christianity. Less evident is the fact that the decline of respect for Christianity brought about changes in all the other categories. The one which suffered the most, after religion, was the area of morality, despite a constant effort to protect that area while attacking religion. The reason, to be sure, is fairly clear. It was the function of the Church to control morality. [Pierre] Bayle [1647–1706] thought that the Church could return that function to the state and morality would not suffer. That idea proved to be untenable. It was thought also by many that the state should control the organization of the Church. That idea produced greater confusion in the state. Nonetheless, politics as a category became, with the weakening of religion, enormously important and in time threatened to take over religion. It is evident that in the Enlightenment proper, it was the most active of the categories. . . .

Thus at the moment of disintegration of the Enlightenment ideal, what really collapsed first was religion and morality. The forces which dominated were political and economic, scientific and esthetic, individualistic and collectivist.

The Wisdom of the Philosophes

I have assumed that it would be wise, if possible, to adopt one particular philosophe from among the group of outstanding ones as the leader of the whole philosophical movement. That is what we have been inclined to do in the past, due in large part to the sheer impossibilty of investigating the operations of all of them. I quickly learned that it would be an injudicious move to select the world of any one of these giants to the exclusion of the concept of the worlds of the others. . . . Voltaire concluded that the human mind was responsible for the making of civilization—total civilization. I judge this conclusion the most significant of all those proposed during the Enlightenment. It was at the core of the notion that enlightenment opens up awareness of the surrounding universe and leads to an augmented happiness. . . . But significant though it was in the making of the Enlightenment, Voltaire was unprepared to carry it out without the notion of

The Global Impact of the Enlightenment

The profound and enduring significance of the Enlightenment is emphasized by Jonathan I. Israel, critically acclaimed historian. He argues that the Enlightenment should be assessed not only in a European but in a global context. When the Enlightenment transformed Europe, it unleashed powerful forces directed toward achieving equality and democracy, forces that are still operative throughout the modern world.

Neither the Enlightenment itself, and still less its consequences, were limited to Europe. There is indeed a further dimension to the problem of how to interpret the Enlightenment. For if the Enlightenment marks the most dramatic step towards secularization and rationalization in Europe's history, it does so no less in the wider history not just of western civilization but, arguably, of the entire world. From this, it plainly follows, it was one of the most important shifts in the history of man. Fittingly, there exists a vast and formidable literature on the topic. Yet there are comparatively few general surveys and large-scale interpretative works, and it is possible to question whether it really receives the emphasis it deserves in the study and teaching of modern history, in comparison, for example, with the Renaissance and the Reformation. These too, of course, were vast and fundamental

Rousseau that civilization always springs, not from the mind, but from the heart of man. What must first be accomplished is that a new science must be created: the science of man. To understand the importance of these categories, one must first seek what is the dynamic relationship of man with all the categories of his existence. Diderot would agree undoubtedly with both of these interpretations, but he would assert that what was more indispensable still was a more profound recognition of the power of change, in which all human possibilities are contained. Really, in his eclectic interpretation of the world, the maker, the supreme poet, is the Great God Change. Change is the full esthetic act. That act demands the human mind of Voltaire, the human heart of Rousseau, and finally, the human creativity of Diderot. The heirs of this

changes, at any rate in western civilization. Nevertheless, these earlier great cultural movements limited as they were to western and central Europe, are really only adjustments, modifications to what was essentially still a theologically conceived and ordered regional society, based on hierarchy and ecclesiastical authority, not universality and equality.

By contrast, the Enlightenment—European and global—not only attacked and severed the roots of traditional European culture in the sacred, magic, kingship, and hierarchy, secularizing all institutions and ideas, but (intellectually and to a degree in practice) effectively demolished all legitimation of monarchy, aristocracy, woman's subordination to man, ecclesiastical authority, and slavery, replacing these with the principles of universality, equality, and democracy. This implies the Enlightenment was of a different order of importance for understanding the rise of the modern world than the Reformation and Renaissance, and that there, is something disproportionate and inadequate about its coverage in the existing historiography [the theory and principles of historical research].

Jonathan I. Israel, preface to *Radical Enlightenment: Philosophy and the Making of Modernity 1650–1750*. Oxford, UK: Oxford University Press, 2001; paper ed. 2002, pp. vi–vii.

new era (this insight into the limitless human possibilities) must incorporate these three insights into an essential new human vision of man's world. The incorporation of any one of these three new worlds requires as much "suspension of disbelief" as the acceptance of God's world. That very act is simultaneously a philosophical and a poetic act, and probably the religious act also. It was, if I have seen things aright, the essential and ultimate human act—terrifyingly complicated, ambiguous, self-contradictory. Voltaire foresaw that the goal is reached through "philosopher" and "poétiser" [writing philosophy and poetry]; through them, one arrives at the making of an acceptable human civilization. Though responsible for the making of the blueprint, Voltaire alone couldn't succeed in putting it into effect. For that, he needed the active collaboration of both Rousseau and Diderot to achieve the ultimate goal.

Did the three of them and all their many followers achieve their goal? Obviously, the answer depends upon the way each of us assess success. . . . We all agree that the Enlightenment terminated in the French Revolution. I added . . . that the dominant trait of Enlightenment thought was its discovery that the ultimate goal of man was the making of a satisfactory civilization in this world. Now I add that two ingredients are most necessary to that end: "*philosopher*" and "*poétiser*"—rational penetration of reality and creative art. Further, every category of human existence is characterized by thought, change, and poetry. If one will learn how to live with ideas (living ideas) and with poetry (harmonious, creative ideas), if he will carefully and scrupulously make an effort to organize (Diderot's great word), order (Rousseau's great word) and examine (Voltaire's great word) he could presumably succeed in making for himself and his society a very enjoyable place to live out quietly his meaning. However, he has not done so yet, not even in "his" world.

Appendix of Documents

Document 1: A Foreigner's Impression of France

Charles-Louis de Secondat, Baron de Montesquieu (1689–1755), editor of the prestigious Encyclopedia *and author of* Spirit of the Laws, *also wrote* Persian Letters, *published in 1721. A fictional work of travel literature, it appealed to French readers because of their fascination with other cultures. Accounts of voyages of exploration and discovery were popular at that time, particularly descriptions of journeys to the exotic East. The* Persian Letters *is composed of a series of 161 letters, many written by two Persian travelers—the Sultan Usbek and his friend and companion Rica—during their extended visit to France (and briefer sojourns in other European countries); also included are replies from people in Persia. The use of letters is a fictional device that enables Montesquieu to appraise various aspects of French society—its manners, morals, religion, economy, and government—through the eyes of a foreigner and thus offer a critical commentary on what he observes. In the following letter, Rica writes his friend Usbek in Smyrna and describes some of the mystifying differences between France and Persia.*

We have been this month at *Paris,* and have hardly been out of motion an hour: it is no small hurry a man must be in before he can get a lodging, find all the people he has directions to, and provide himself with all the Necessaries which he must have about him immediately.

Paris is as large as *Ispahan:* the Houses are so high that you wou'd swear they were all built for Astrologers. Thou wilt easily judge that a City built in the air and that has six or seven houses one at the top of the other, must be extremely populous, and that when all the folks are come down into the street there must be a blessed crowd and hurry.

Thou wilt hardly believe it; for this month that I have been here I have not yet seen any body walk: there is no people under the sun that get so much work out of their machine as the *French:* they run; they fly: the slow carriages of *Asia,* the regular step of our Camels, wou'd lay them to sleep. As for me, who am not used to this sport, and who often go on foot my old pace, I am sometimes made as mad as a Christian: for not to insist upon my being all splashed from head to foot, I can never forgive the punches of elbows which I receive regularly and periodically: one man that comes behind me and out-walks me, gives me a whisk half round, and another that crosses me on t'other side, twirls me again in a moment into my right place again; so that in a hundred paces I am more battered and bruised than if I had walked thirty mile.

Do not imagine I can as yet give thee any thorow description of the Manners and Customs of these *Europeans:* I have but a slight notion of them my self, having yet had but just time to Wonder.

The King of *France* [Louis XIV] is the most potent Prince in *Europe:* he has no Gold Mines like his neighbour the King of *Spain*; but he has more Wealth than him, as he raises it out of the vanity of his Subjects, which is more inexhaustible than any Mine: He has undertaken and maintained great Wars upon no other Fund but the Sale of Titles of Honour: and by a Prodigy of humane Pride, his Troops were paid, his Places fortified and his Fleets equipped.

Besides, this Prince is a great Magician: he exercises dominion even over the minds of his Subjects: he makes them think just as he wou'd have them: If he has but one million of Crowns in his Treasury, and stands in need of two, he only bids them believe that one Crown is Two, and they believe it. If he has a difficult War to support and has no Money at all, he only puts it into their heads that paper is money, and they are presently convinced that it is so: nay he often makes them believe that he cures them of all distempers by touching them, so great is the influence and power which he has over their Minds.

What I tell thee of this Prince need not surprize thee: there is another Magician stronger than him, who is master of his mind no less than he is of the minds of the others. This Magician is called the *Pope:* at one time he makes him believe that three are but one [the Trinity]: that the bread he eats is not bread, or that the wine he drinks is not wine [the Catholic belief in transubstantiation— the conversion of bread and wine into the body and blood of Christ], and a thousand strange things of that nature.

Charles-Louis de Montesquieu, *Persian Letters*, trans. John Ozell. London, 1722. Facsimile edition, New York: Garland, 1972, Vol. I: pp. 78–81. Language and spelling have been modernized by editor.

Document 2: Swift's Satiric View of England

Jonathan Swift's Travels into Several Remote Nations of the World, *published anonymously in 1726, purports to be the account of four sea voyages undertaken by Lemuel Gulliver, an Englishman who served as ship's surgeon and then captain. Adopting the format of the popular travel book, Swift transformed the fantastic and allegorical adventures of Gulliver into a biting satire on human vice and the corrup-*

tion of England as well as that of eighteenth-century Europe. The following passage is taken from Gulliver's second voyage—to Brobdingnag, land of giants. Gulliver has just given a detailed explanation of British political and judicial institutions to the king of the Brobdingnagians.

[The king] was perfectly astonished with the historical account I gave him of our affairs during the last century; protesting it was only a heap of conspiracies, rebellions, murders, massacres, revolutions, banishments; the very worst effects that avarice, faction, hypocrisy, perfidiousness, cruelty, rage, madness, hatred, envy, lust, malice, and ambition could produce.

His Majesty in another audience, was at the pains to recapitulate the sum of all I had spoken; compared the questions he made, with the answers I had given; then taking me into his hands, and stroaking me gently, delivered himself in these words, which I shall never forget, nor the manner he spoke them in. 'My little friend [Gulliver]; you have made a most admirable panegyrick [speech of praise] upon your country. You have clearly proved that ignorance, idleness, and vice, are the proper ingredients for qualifying a legislator. That laws are best explained, interpreted, and applied by those whose interest and abilities lie in perverting, confounding, and eluding them. I observe among you, some lines of an institution, which in its original might have been tolerable; but these half erased, and the rest wholly blurred and blotted by corruptions. It doth not appear, from all you have said, how any one perfection is required, from towards the procurement of any one station among you; much less that men are ennobled on account of their virtue, that priests are advanced for their piety or learning, soldiers for their conduct or valour, judges for their integrity, senators for the love of their country, or counsellors for their wisdom. As for yourself (continued the king) who have spent the greatest part of your life in travelling; I am well disposed to hope you may hitherto have escaped many vices of your country. But, by what I have gathered from your own relation, and the answers I have with much pains wringed and extorted from you; I cannot but conclude the bulk of your natives, to be the most pernicious race of little odious vermin that nature ever suffered to crawl upon the surface of the earth.'

Jonathan Swift, *Gulliver's Travels*. London: J.M. Dent & Sons, 1906. Reprinted 1975, pp. 139–40.

Document 3: Locke on the Origins of Human Society

The writings of the renowned English philosopher John Locke (1632–1704) influenced political thought in Britain, France, and America during

the Enlightenment. In the following selection from the Second Treatise of
Civil Government, *published in 1689, Locke contrasts two stages of socio-
political development. He contends that since human beings are free, equal,
and independent in their natural state, they must willingly consent to give
up their autonomy when they join together to form a community.*

Men being, as has been said, by nature all free, equal, and independent, no one can be put out of this estate and subjected to the political power of another without his own consent, which is done by
agreeing with other men, to join and unite into a community for
their comfortable, safe, and peaceable living, one amongst another,
in a secure enjoyment of their properties, and a greater security
against any that are not of it. This any number of men may do, because it injures not the freedom of the rest; they are left, as they
were, in the liberty of the state of Nature. When any number of men
have so consented to make one community or government, they are
thereby presently incorporated, and make one body politic, wherein
the majority have a right to act and conclude the rest. . . .

Whosoever, therefore, out of a state of Nature unite into a
community, must be understood to give up all the power necessary
to the ends for which they unite into society to the majority of the
community, unless they expressly agreed in any number greater
than the majority. And this is done by barely agreeing to unite into
one political society, which is all the compact that is, or needs be,
between the individuals that enter into or make up a commonwealth. And thus, that which begins and actually constitutes any political society is nothing but the consent of any number of freemen
capable of majority, to unite and incorporate into such a society.
And this is that, and that only, which did or could give beginning to
any lawful government in the world.

John Locke, *Second Treatise of Civil Government,* in *Two Treatises of Civil Government.* London:
J.M. Dent & Sons, 1924. Reprinted 1949, pp. 164–66.

Document 4: Rousseau on *The Social Contract*

*Like John Locke, Jean-Jacques Rousseau (1712–1778) traces the socio-
political development of man. Rousseau's* The Social Contract, *published
in 1762, is a seminal text in political philosophy. In the following excerpt
from this work, Rousseau analyzes the function of the social contract, show-
ing how it enables man to make the transition from an unfettered state of
nature to a "civil state" in which people cooperate for their mutual benefit.*

Man is born free; and everywhere he is in chains. One thinks himself the master of others, and still remains a greater slave than they.

How did this change come about? I do not know. What can make it legitimate? That question I think I can answer.

If I took into account only force, and the effects derived from it, I should say: 'As long as a people is compelled to obey, and obeys, it does well; as soon as it can shake off the yoke, and shakes it off, it does still better; for, regaining its liberty by the same right as took it away, either it is justified in resuming it, or there was no justification for those who took it away.' But the social order is a sacred right which is the basis of all other rights. Nevertheless, this right does not come from nature, and must therefore be founded on conventions [mutual agreements]. . . .

THE SOCIAL COMPACT

I suppose men to have reached the point at which the obstacles in the way of their preservation in the state of nature show their power of resistance to be greater than the resources at the disposal of each individual for his maintenance in that state. That primitive condition can then subsist no longer; and the human race would perish unless it changed its manner of existence.

But, as men cannot engender new forces, but only unite and direct existing ones, they have no other means of preserving themselves than the formation, by aggregation, of a sum of forces great enough to overcome the resistance. These they have to bring into play by means of a single motive power, and cause to act in concert.

This sum of forces can arise only where several persons come together: but, as the force and liberty of each man are the chief instruments of his self-preservation, how can he pledge them without harming his own interests, and neglecting the care he owes to himself? This difficulty, in its bearing on my present subject, may be stated in the following terms:

'The problem is to find a form of association which will defend and protect with the whole common force the person and goods of each associate, and in which each, while uniting himself with all, may still obey himself alone, and remain as free as before.' This is the fundamental problem of which the *Social Contract* provides the solution.

The clauses of this contract are so determined by the nature of the act that the slightest modification would make them vain and ineffective; so that, although they have perhaps never been formally set forth, they are everywhere the same and everywhere tacitly admitted and recognized, until, on the violation of the social compact, each regains his original rights and resumes his natural liberty, while losing the conventional liberty in favour of which he renounced it.

These clauses, properly understood, may be reduced to one—the total alienation of each associate, together with all his rights, to the whole community; for, in the first place, as each gives himself absolutely, the conditions are the same for all; and, this being so, no one has any interest in making them burdensome to others.

Moreover, the alienation being without reserve, the union is as perfect as it can be, and no associate has anything more to demand: for, if the individuals retained certain rights, as there would be no common superior to decide between them and the public, each, being on one point his own judge, would ask to be so on all; the state of nature would thus continue, and the association would necessarily become inoperative or tyrannical.

Finally, each man, in giving himself to all, gives himself to nobody; and as there is no associate over which he does not acquire the same right as he yields others over himself, he gains an equivalent for everything he loses, and an increase of force for the preservation of what he has.

If then we discard from the social compact what is not of its essence, we shall find that it reduces itself to the following terms:

'Each of us puts his person and all his power in common under the supreme direction of the general will, and, in our corporate capacity, we receive each member as an indivisible part of the whole.'

At once, in place of the individual personality of each contracting party, this act of association creates a moral and collective body, composed of as many members as the assembly contains voters, and receiving from this act its unity, its common identity, its life, and its will. This public person, so formed by the union of all other persons, formerly took the name of *city*, and now takes that of *Republic* or *body politic*; it is called by its members *State* when passive, *Sovereign* when active, and *Power* when compared with others like itself. Those who are associated in it take collectively the name of *people*, and severally are called *citizens*, as sharing in the sovereign power, and *subjects*, as being under the laws of the State.

Jean-Jacques Rousseau, *The Social Contract*, in *The Social Contract and Discourses*, trans. G.D.H. Cole. London: J.M. Dent & Sons, 1913. Reprinted 1952, pp. 3–4, 11–13.

Document 5: Kant Defines "Enlightenment"

Immanuel Kant (1724–1804), the great German philosopher of the Enlightenment, analyzed the contribution that reason and experience each made to human knowledge, as can be seen in his most celebrated work, the

Critique of Pure Reason, *published in 1781. Several years later, in 1784, he published his essay,* An Answer to the Question: What Is Enlightenment?, *from which the following excerpt is taken. Here Kant sets forth the prerequisites essential for enlightenment, among them the pursuit of knowledge, the use of reason, and freedom of speech and thought.*

Enlightenment is mankind's exit from its self-incurred immaturity. Immaturity is the inability to make use of one's own understanding without the guidance of another. *Self-incurred* is this inability if its cause lies not in the lack of understanding but rather in the lack of the resolution and the courage to use it without the guidance of another. *Sapere aude!* [Dare to know!] Have the courage to use your *own* understanding! is thus the motto of enlightenment.

Laziness and cowardice are the reasons why such a great part of mankind . . . still gladly remain immature for life and why it is so easy for others to set themselves up as guardians. It is so easy to be immature. . . .

It is thus difficult for any individual man to work himself out of an immaturity that has become almost natural to him. He has become fond of it and, for the present, is truly incapable of making use of his own reason, because he has never been permitted to make the attempt. Rules and formulas, these mechanical instruments of a rational use (or rather misuse) of his natural gifts, are the fetters of an everlasting immaturity. Whoever casts them off would still take but an uncertain leap over the smallest ditch, because he is not accustomed to such free movement. Hence there are only a few who have managed to free themselves from immaturity through the exercise of their own minds, and yet proceed confidently. . . .

For this enlightenment, however, nothing more is required than *freedom;* and indeed the most harmless form of all the things that may be called freedom: namely, the freedom to make a *public use* of one's reason in all matters.

Immanuel Kant, *An Answer to the Question: What Is Enlightenment?*, trans. James Schmidt, in *What is Enlightenment? Eighteenth-Century Answers and Twentieth-Century Questions*, ed. James Schmidt. Berkeley: University of California Press, 1996, pp. 58–59.

Document 6: A Call to Americans to Revolt

British by birth but American by choice, Thomas Paine (1737–1809) was an ardent advocate of revolution. He wrote several polemical political tracts, including Common Sense, *published in 1776, in support of the American Revolution and* The Rights of Man, *published in 1791 and 1792, in defense of the French Revolution. In the following passages taken from* Common Sense, *Paine extols the "glorious" ideal of liberty.*

As he addresses his countrymen on the very eve of revolution, he sounds a clarion cry, urging his fellow Americans to free themselves from the yoke of British tyranny and oppression.

A government of our own is our natural right; and when a man seriously reflects on the precariousness of human affairs, he will become convinced that it is infinitely wiser and safer to form a constitution of our own in a cool, deliberate manner, while we have it in our power, than to trust such an interesting event to time and chance. If we omit it now, some [popular leader] may hereafter arise, who, laying hold of popular disquietudes, may collect together the desperate and discontented, and, by assuming to themselves the powers of government, may sweep away the liberties of the continent like a deluge. Should the government of America return again to the hands of Britain, the tottering situation of things will be a temptation for some desperate adventurer to try his fortune; and in such a case, what relief can Britain give? Ere she could hear the news, the fatal business might be done; and ourselves suffering, like the wretched Britons, under the oppression of the conqueror. Ye that oppose independence now, ye know not what ye do; ye are opening a door to eternal tyranny, by keeping vacant the seat of government.

There are thousands and tens of thousands who would think it glorious to expel from the continent that barbarous and hellish power which hath stirred up the Indians and negroes to destroy us; the cruelty hath a double guilt, it is dealing brutally by us and treacherously by them.

To talk of friendship with those in whom our reason forbids us to have faith, and our affections, wounded through a thousand pores, instruct us to detest, is madness and folly. Every day wears out the little remains of kindred between us and them, and can there be any reason to hope that, as the relationship expires, the affection will increase? or that we shall agree better when we have ten times more and greater concerns to quarrel over than ever?

Ye that tell us of harmony and reconciliation, can ye restore to us the time that is past? Can ye give to prostitution its former innocence? Neither can ye reconcile Britain and America. The last cord now is broken, the people of England are presenting addresses against us. There are injuries which nature cannot forgive; she would cease to be nature if she did. As well can the lover forgive the ravisher of his mistress as the continent forgive the murderers of Britain. The Almighty hath implanted in us these unextinguishable feelings for good and wise purposes.

They are the guardians of his image in our hearts. They distinguish us from the herd of common animals. The social compact would dissolve, and justice be extirpated from the earth, or have only a casual existence, were we callous to the touches of affection. The robber and the murderer would often escape unpunished, did not the injuries which our temper sustains provoke us into justice.

O! ye that love mankind! Ye that dare oppose, not only the tyranny, but the tyrant, stand forth! Every spot of the old world is overrun with oppression. Freedom hath been hunted round the globe. Asia and Africa have long expelled her, Europe regards her like a stranger, and England hath given her warning to depart. O! receive the fugitive; and prepare in time an asylum for mankind.

Thomas Paine, *Common Sense*. Reprinted in Thomas Paine, *Paine's Political Writings During the American and French Revolutions*, ed. Hypatia Bradlaugh Bronner. London: Watts, 1909, pp. 25–26.

Document 7: The American Declaration of Independence

The Declaration of Independence, written by Thomas Jefferson, was signed by representatives of all thirteen American colonies and passed unanimously by Congress on July 4, 1776. In this historic document, the colonists repudiated all allegiance to the British crown and, in effect, asserted their government's right to declare revolution as a legitimate means of securing the freedom and happiness of its citizens. The Americans thus put into practice many of the political and philosophical ideas of the French Enlightenment. The American Revolution, in turn, subsequently helped to inspire the French Revolution in 1789.

When in the course of human events it becomes necessary for one people to dissolve the political bands which have connected them with another, and to assume among the powers of the earth, the separate and equal station to which the Laws of Nature and of Nature's God entitle them, a decent respect to the opinions of mankind requires that they should declare the causes which impel them to the separation.

We hold these truths to be self-evident, that all men are created equal, that they are endowed by their Creator with certain unalienable rights, that among these are life, liberty and the pursuit of happiness. That to secure these rights, governments are instituted among men, deriving their just powers from the consent of the governed. That whenever any form of government becomes destructive of these ends, it is the right of the people to alter or to abolish it, and to institute new government, laying its foundation on such principles and organizing its powers in such form, as to them shall seem most likely to effect their safety and happiness. Prudence, indeed, will dictate that governments long established should not be changed for light and transient causes; and accordingly all experience hath shown, that mankind are more disposed to suffer, while evils are sufferable, than to right themselves by abolishing the forms to which they are accustomed. But when a long train of abuses and usurpations, pursuing invariably the same object, evinces a design to reduce them under absolute despotism, it is their right, it is their duty, to throw off such government, and to provide new guards for their future security. Such has been the patient sufferance of these Colonies; and such is now the necessity which constrains them to alter their former systems of government. The history of the present King of Great Britain is a history of repeated injuries and usurpations, all having, in direct object, the establishment of an absolute tyranny over these States. . . .

In every stage of these oppressions we have petitioned for redress in the most humble terms: our repeated petitions have been answered only by repeated injury. A prince whose character is thus marked by every act which may define a tyrant is unfit to be the ruler of a free people.

Nor have we been wanting in attention to our British brethren. We have warned them from time to time of attempts by their legislature to extend an unwarrantable jurisdiction over us. We have reminded them of the circumstances of our emigration and settlement here. We have appealed to their native justice and magnanimity, and we have conjured them by the ties of our common kindred to disavow these usurpations, which would inevitably interrupt our connections and correspondence. They too have been deaf to the voice of justice and of consanguinity. We must, therefore, acquiesce in the necessity, which denounces our separation, and hold them, as we hold the rest of mankind, enemies in war, in peace, friends.

We, therefore, the Representatives of the United States of America, in General Congress assembled, appealing to the Supreme Judge of the world for the rectitude of our intentions, do, in the name, and by authority of the good people of these Colonies, solemnly publish and declare, That these United Colonies are, and of right ought to be, Free and Independent States; that they are absolved from all allegiance to the British Crown, and that all political connection between them and the State of Great Britain, is and ought to be totally dissolved; and that as Free and Independent States, they have full power to levy war, conclude peace, contract alliances, establish commerce, and to do all other acts and things which Independent States may of right do. And for the support of this declaration, with a firm reliance on the protection of Divine Providence, we mutually pledge to each other our lives, our fortunes, and our sacred honor.

Thomas Jefferson, The Declaration of Independence, in *The Book of Great American Documents*, ed. Vincent Wilson Jr., 3rd ed. Brookeville, MD: American History Research Associates, 1998, pp. 15–18.

Document 8: A Charter of Human Rights

As U.S. envoy to France, Thomas Jefferson (1743–1826) observed the turmoil in the months preceding the French Revolution and even attended the futile deliberations of the Estates-General in Versailles, on May 5, 1789. Convinced though he was of the legitimacy of the French citizens' grievances against their king, Jefferson nonetheless made an effort to avert disaster by proposing that a formal charter of rights be adopted and promulgated by the king.

In the following excerpt from his Autobiography, *written in 1821 at the age of 77, Jefferson recalls his experiences in France. He alludes to the Charter of Rights that he had urged King Louis XVI to adopt just before the outbreak of revolution and comments on the disastrous consequences of the French monarch's failure to do so.*

I considered a successful reformation of government in France, as ensuring a general reformation thro Europe, and the resurrection, to a new life, of their people, now ground to dust by the abuses of the governing powers. I was much acquainted with the leading patriots of the assembly. Being from a country which had successfully passed thro' a similar reformation, they were disposed to my acquaintance, and had some confidence in me. I urged most strenuously an immediate compromise; to secure what the government was now ready to yield, and trust to future occasions for what might still be wanting. It was well understood that the King would grant at this time 1. Freedom of the person by Habeas corpus. 2. Freedom of conscience. 3. Freedom of the press. 4. Trial by jury. 5. A representative legislature. 6. Annual meetings. 7. The origination of laws. 8. The exclusive right of taxation and appropriation. And 9. The responsibility of ministers; and with the exercise of these powers they would obtain in future whatever might be further necessary to improve and preserve their constitution. They thought otherwise however, and events have proved their lamentable error. For after 30 years of war, foreign and domestic, the loss of millions of lives, the prostration of private happiness, and foreign subjugation of their own country for a time, they have obtained no more, nor even that securely. They were unconscious of (for who could foresee?) the melancholy sequel of their well-meant perseverance; that their physical force would be usurped by a first tyrant to trample on the independence, and even the existence, of other nations: that this would afford fatal example for the atrocious conspiracy of Kings against their people; would generate their unholy and homicide alliance to make common cause among themselves, and to crush, by the power of the whole, the efforts of any part, to moderate their abuses and oppressions.

Thomas Jefferson, *Autobiography*, in *Writings: Autobiography, Notes on the State of Virginia, Public and Private Papers, Addresses, Letters*. New York: The Library of America, 1984, pp. 85–86.

Document 9: Defending Freedom of the Press

Carl Friedrich Bahrdt (1740–1792) was a German theologian whose views were so liberal, even radical, that they offended both church and state. Bahrdt was imprisoned for a year for writing political satire and later banned for heresy, in both instances by the Imperial Edict of Frederick the Great of Prussia. The following extract is from his work On Freedom of the Press, *published anonymously in 1787.*

THE FREEDOM TO SPEAK AND TO WRITE IS A UNIVERSAL RIGHT OF MAN

The freedom to share one's insights and judgments verbally or in writing is, just like the freedom to think, a holy and inviolable right of man that, as a universal right of man, is above all the rights of princes. And the regent who says that he leaves it to each to hold his own opinion and to believe what he wants, but that he may not speak or write what he wants, plays with human understanding and takes mankind for fools. Because basically that is saying no more and no less than: "I will permit you to do what I cannot prevent, but I will take away this facetious permission by preventing you and the rest of mankind from enjoying it." Judge impartially and tell me if this is the case. Can a prince, if he has half a million soldiers standing ready to execute his orders, coerce my understanding? Can he influence the inner workings of my soul? Can he prevent me from thinking, judging, or believing something? Oh, proud impotence! And still he will take the liberty to say, "I permit my subjects to believe what they will." Is it not foolish to reckon as a favor what is a necessity? And is not this gracious permission as curious as if a master wished to pay his servants with the seven days of the week and, indeed, free light during daytime? No, dear rulers, you must not toy with men who are only different from you by accident. . . . You must remember that the right to think (thank God!) is not within your jurisdiction; that you are not permitting anything if you rob us of the right to speak, and that you trample underfoot all the rights of mankind if one of them is not sacred to you.

Carl Friedrich Bahrdt, *On Freedom of the Press and Its Limits: For Consideration by Rulers, Censors, and Writers*, trans. John Christian Laursen, in *What Is Enlightenment? Eighteenth-Century Answers and Twentieth-Century Questions*, ed. James Schmidt. Berkeley: University of California Press, 1996, pp. 100–101.

Document 10: A Plea for Tolerance

François-Marie Arouet de Voltaire (1694–1778) was a skeptic who rejected organized religion. Convinced that religious disputes caused wars throughout history, Voltaire deplored the cruelty and injustice perpetrated through the ages in the name of religion, and he condemned the fanatic persecution of anyone who dared question the religious dogma of the established church. In his Treatise on Tolerance, *published in 1763 and excerpted below, Voltaire focuses particular attention on the treatment of the French Protestants (or Huguenots) by the Catholic Church. Since 1685, when Louis XIV had revoked the Edict of Nantes, which had safeguarded the rights of French Protestants for almost a hundred years, they had suffered harsh penalties. Voltaire argues for an enlightened and humane religious policy of toleration on the part of king and church, maintaining that members of other religions, including Protestants, should be allowed to live their lives in peace without fear of persecution.*

Everywhere government has become stronger and society gentler. Police forces, supported by extensive regular armies, ensure that we need not fear a return of those anarchic times when Calvinist peasants fought Catholic peasants in scratch militias put together between seed-time and harvest.

A new age must bring new attitudes. It would be absurd to punish the Sorbonne today for having in the past petitioned to burn Joan of Arc, or declared that Henri III forfeited his right to reign, or excommunicated and banished the great Henri IV. Just as ridiculous would it be to root out those other establishments once guilty of excess in times of madness. Such would not only be unjust, it would contain about as much sense as to subject the entire population of Marseilles to a wholesale medical cure today because they had been visited by the plague in 1720. . . .

And so the history of our entire continent gives proof that it is foolish either to promulgate religious intolerance or to base policy upon it. . . .

In the end, tolerance has been responsible for not a single civil war, whereas intolerance has covered the earth with corpses.

François-Marie Arouet de Voltaire, *Treatise of Tolerance*, trans. Brian Masters, in *Voltaire: Treatise on Tolerance and Other Writings*, ed. Simon Harvey. Cambridge, UK: Cambridge University Press, 2000, pp. 18–19, 22.

Document 11: Paine Attacks Religion

Thomas Paine (1737–1809) was one of the most radical and controversial figures of his time. Born in England, Paine immigrated to America where he became a fervent revolutionary who, intent on overthrowing the established political authority, supported both the American and the French revolutions. Paine also repudiated traditional religious authority as can be seen in The Age of Reason, *published in two parts in 1794 and 1796. In this attack on established religion, excerpted below, he derides religious superstition and sets out to prove that religion contradicts reason—a point of view often expressed by the French* philosophes.

I believe in one God, and no more; and I hope for happiness beyond this life.

I believe in the equality of man, and I believe that religious duties consist in doing justice, loving mercy, and endeavouring to make our fellow-creatures happy.

But lest it should be supposed that I believe many other things in addition to these, I shall, in the progress of this work, declare the things I do not believe, and my reasons for not believing them.

I do not believe in the creed professed by the Jewish Church, by the Roman Church, by the Greek Church, by the Turkish Church, by the Protestant Church, nor by any Church that I know of. My own mind is my own church.

All national institutions of Churches, whether Jewish, Christian, or Turkish, appear to me no other than human inventions set up to terrify and enslave mankind, and monopolise power and profit.

I do not mean by this declaration to condemn those who believe otherwise. They have the same right to their belief as I have to mine. But it is necessary to the happiness of man that he be mentally faithful to himself. Infidelity does not consist in believing or in disbelieving; it consists in professing to believe what he does not believe.

It is impossible to calculate the moral mischief, if I may so express it, that mental lying has produced in society. When a man has so far corrupted and prostituted the chastity of his mind as to subscribe his professional belief in things he does not believe, he has prepared himself for the commission of every other crime. He takes up the trade of a priest for the sake of gain, and, in order to *qualify* himself for that trade, he begins with a perjury. Can we conceive anything more destructive to morality than this? . . .

Every national Church or religion has established itself by pretending some special mission from God, communicated to certain individuals. The Jews have their Moses; the Christians their Jesus Christ, their apostles and saints; and the Turks their Mahomet; as if the way to God was not open to every man alike.

Each of those Churches show certain books which they call *revelation*, or the word of God. The Jews say that their word of God was given by God to Moses face to face; the Christians say that their word of God came by divine inspiration; and the Turks say that their word of God (the Koran) was brought by an angel from heaven. Each of those Churches accuses the other of unbelief; and, for my own part, I disbelieve them all.

As it is necessary to affix right ideas to words, I will, before I proceed further into the subject, offer some observations on the word *revelation*. Revelation, when applied to religion, means something communicated *immediately* from God to man.

No one will deny or dispute the power of the Almighty to make such a communication if he pleases. But admitting, for the sake of a case, that something has been revealed to a certain person, and not revealed to any other person, it is revelation to that person only. When he tells it to a second person, a second to a third, a third to a fourth, and so on, it ceases to be a revelation to all those persons. It is revelation to the first person only, and *hearsay* to every other; and consequently they are not obliged to believe it.

It is a contradiction in terms and ideas to call anything a revelation that comes to us at second hand, either verbally or in writing. Revelation is necessarily limited to the first communication. After this it is only an account of something which that person says was a revelation to him; and though he may find himself obliged to believe it, it cannot be incumbent on me to believe it in the same manner, for it was not a revelation made to *me*, and I have only his word for it that it was made to him.

Thomas Paine, *The Age of Reason.* Reprint, ed. Hypatia Bradlaugh Bonner. London: Watts, [1909?], Part 1. pp. 1–2.

Document 12: A Denial of the Existence of God

Paul Heinrich Dietrich, Baron d'Holbach (1723–1789) was a German nobleman and intellectual who lived in Paris and hosted a salon where the philosophes *and eminent thinkers of the time exchanged ideas. D'Holbach's religious views were even more radical than those of Voltaire, for he was an avowed atheist. In the following passages from his book* Good . . . Sense, or

Natural Ideas vs. Supernatural Ideas, *published in 1772, he sets forth his defense of atheism, refuting various arguments for the existence of God.*

REFUTATION OF ARGUMENTS
FOR THE EXISTENCE OF GOD

Ignorance and fear are the two hinges of all religion. The uncertainty in which man finds himself in relation to his God, is precisely the motive that attaches him to his religion. Man is fearful in the dark—in moral, as well as physical darkness. His fear becomes habitual, and habit makes it natural; he would think that he wanted something, if he had nothing to fear.

In point of religion, men are only great children. The more a religion is absurd, and filled with wonders, the greater ascendancy it acquires over them. The devout man thinks himself obliged to place no bounds to his credulity; the more things are inconceivable, they appear to him divine; the more they are incredible, the greater merit he imagines, there is in believing them.

Paul Heinrich Dietrich d'Holbach, *Good (or Common) Sense, or Natural Ideas vs. Supernatural Ideas*, trans. H.D. Robinson, in *Eighteenth-Century Philosophy*, ed. Lewis White Beck. New York: The Free Press, 1966, pp. 182–83.

Document 13: Wordsworth Enthusiastically Supports the French Revolution

William Wordsworth (1770–1850), the great English Romantic poet, visited France in 1790, after completing university, and then spent a year living there (1791–1792). He witnessed at firsthand the revolutionary fervor and hope for a better future and, with the idealism of youth, rejoiced in what he thought would be the triumph of liberal political ideals: "Bliss was it in that dawn to be alive." This well-known line is taken from the following poem, "French Revolution," which records Wordsworth's feelings about this historic event. The poem was written in 1804, after his return to England, and published in 1809.

FRENCH REVOLUTION

Oh! pleasant exercise of hope and joy!
For mighty were the auxiliars which then stood
Upon our side, we who were strong in love!
Bliss was it in that dawn to be alive,
But to be young was very heaven!—Oh! times,
In which the meagre, stale, forbidding ways
Of custom, law, and statute, took at once
The attraction of a country in romance!
When Reason seemed the most to assert her rights,
When most intent on making of herself

A prime Enchantress—to assist the work
Which then was going forward in her name!
Not favoured spots alone, but the whole earth,
The beauty wore of promise, that which sets
(As at some moment might not be unfelt
Among the bowers of paradise itself)
The budding rose above the rose full blown.
What temper at the prospect did not wake
To happiness unthought of? The inert
Were roused, and lively natures rapt away!
They who had fed their childhood upon dreams
The playfellows of fancy, who had made
All powers of swiftness, subtilty, and strength
Their ministers,—who in lordly wise had stirred
Among the grandest objects of the sense,
And dealt with whatsoever they found there
As if they had within some lurking right
To wield it;—they, too, who, of gentle mood,
Had watched all gentle motions, and to these
Had fitted their own thoughts, schemers more mild,
And in the region of their peaceful selves;—
Now was it that both found, the meek and lofty
Did both find, helpers to their heart's desire,
And stuff at hand, plastic as they could wish;
Were called upon to exercise their skill,
Not in Utopia, subterranean fields,
Or some secreted island, Heaven knows where!
But in the very world, which is the world
Of all of us,—the place where in the end
We find our happiness, or not at all!

William Wordsworth, "French Revolution," in *The Poetical Works of Wordsworth*, ed. Thomas Hutchinson, rev. ed. London: Oxford University Press, 1936, pp. 165–66.

Document 14: The Storming of the Bastille

The storming of the Bastille, the notorious prison in Paris, by an angry, bloodthirsty mob intent on releasing the prisoners, was an act of violence that marked the outbreak of the French Revolution on July 14, 1789. This historical event, imaginatively reconstructed by Charles Dickens, is described vividly in his novel, A Tale of Two Cities, *published in 1859. As shown in the following extract, the citizens of Saint Antoine in Paris are led by the patriots, Monsieur Defarge, owner of a wine shop, and his vicious wife, Madame Defarge.*

Saint Antoine [a district of Paris] had been, that morning, a vast dusky mass of scarecrows heaving to and fro, with frequent gleams of light above the billowy heads, where steel blades and bayonets shone in the sun. A tremendous roar arose from the throat of Saint Antoine, and a forest of naked arms struggled in the air like shrivelled branches of trees in a winter wind: all the fingers convulsively clutching at every weapon or semblance of a weapon that was thrown up from the depths below, no matter how far off.

Who gave them out, whence they last came, where they began, through what agency they crookedly quivered and jerked, scores at a time, over the heads of the crowd, like a kind of lightning, no eye in the throng could have told; but, muskets were being distributed—so were cartridges, powder and ball, bars of iron and wood, knives, axes, pikes, every weapon that distracted ingenuity could discover or devise. People who could lay hold of nothing else, set themselves with bleeding hands to force stones and bricks out of their places in walls. Every pulse and heart in Saint Antoine was on high-fever strain and at high-fever heat. Every living creature there held life as of no account, and was demented with a passionate readiness to sacrifice it.

As a whirlpool of boiling waters has a centre point, so, all this raging circled round [French Revolutionary] Defarge's wine shop, and every human drop in the cauldron had a tendency to be sucked towards the vortex where Defarge himself, already begrimed with gunpowder and sweat, issued orders, issued arms, thrust this man back, dragged this man forward, disarmed one to arm another, laboured and strove in the thickest of the uproar. . . .

'Where is my wife?' [cried Defarge].

'Eh, well! Here you see me!' said madame, composed as ever, but not knitting to-day. Madame's resolute right hand was occupied with an axe, in place of the usual softer implements, and in her girdle were a pistol and a cruel knife.

'Where do you go, my wife?'

'I go,' said madame, 'with you at present. You shall see me at the head of women, by and by.'

'Come then!' cried Defarge, in a resounding voice. 'Patriots and friends, we are ready! The Bastille!' [notorious prison in Paris].

With a roar that sounded as if all the breath in France had been shaped into the detested word, the living sea rose, wave on wave, depth on depth, and overflowed the city to that point. Alarm-bells ringing, drums beating, the sea raging and thundering on its new beach, the attack begun.

Deep ditches, double drawbridge, massive stone walls, eight great towers, cannon, muskets, fire and smoke. Through the fire and through the smoke—in the fire and in the smoke, for the sea cast him up against a cannon, and on the instant he became a cannonier—Defarge of the wine shop worked like a manful soldier, Two fierce hours.

Deep ditch, single drawbridge, massive stone walls, eight great towers, cannon, muskets, fire and smoke. One drawbridge down! 'Work, comrades all, work! Work . . . work!' Thus Defarge of the wine shop, still at his gun, which had long grown hot.

'To me, women!' cried madame his wife. 'What! We can kill as well as the men when the place is taken!' And to her, with a shrill thirsty cry, trooping women variously armed, but all armed alike in hunger and revenge.

Cannon, muskets, fire and smoke; but, still the deep ditch, the single drawbridge, the massive stone walls, and the eight great towers. Slight displacements of the raging sea, made by the falling wounded. Flashing weapons, blazing torches, smoking wagon-loads of wet straw, hard work at neighbouring barricades in all directions, shrieks, volleys, execrations, bravery without stint, boom smash and rattle, and the furious sounding of the living sea; but, still the deep ditch, and the single drawbridge, and the massive stone walls, and the eight great towers, and still Defarge of the wine shop at his gun, grown doubly hot by the service of Four fierce hours.

A white flag from within the fortress, and a parley—this dimly perceptible through the raging storm, nothing audible in it—suddenly the sea rose immeasurably wider and higher and swept Defarge of the wine shop over the lowered drawbridge, past the massive stone outer walls, in among the eight great towers surrendered! . . .

The sea rushed on. The sea of black and threatening waters, and of destructive upheaving of wave against wave, whose depths were yet unfathomed and whose forces were yet unknown. The remorseless sea of turbulently swaying shapes, voices of vengeance, and faces hardened in the furnaces of suffering until the touch of pity could make no mark on them.

Charles Dickens, *A Tale of Two Cities*. London: Dent, 1906. Reprinted 1970, pp. 209–11, 215.

Document 15: Burke Condemns the French Revolution

Although born in Ireland, Edmund Burke (1730–1797), a conservative British politician and writer, was a staunch defender of the British monarchy. He sets forth his ideas on revolution, in general, and on the

French Revolution, in particular, in his well-known essay, "Reflections on the Revolution in France," published in 1790. In the passages quoted below, he describes the excesses of the French Revolution, deploring the anarchy that continued to prevail in France.

France, by the perfidy of her leaders, has utterly disgraced the tone of lenient counsel in the cabinets of princes, and disarmed it of its most potent topics. She has sanctified the dark, suspicious maxims of tyrannous distrust; and taught kings to tremble at (what will hereafter be called) the delusive plausibilities of moral politicians. Sovereigns will consider those, who advise them to place an unlimited confidence in their people, as subverters of their thrones; as traitors who aim at their destruction, by leading their easy good-nature, under specious pretences, to admit combinations of bold and faithless men into a participation of their power. This alone (if there were nothing else) is an irreparable calamity to you and to mankind. Remember that your parliament of Paris told your king, that, in calling the states together, he had nothing to fear but the prodigal excess of their zeal in providing for the support of the throne. It is right that these men should hide their heads. It is right that they should bear their part in the ruin which their counsel has brought on their sovereign and their country. Such sanguine declarations tend to lull authority asleep; to encourage it rashly to engage in perilous adventures of untried policy; to neglect those provisions, preparations and precautions, which distinguish benevolence from imbecility; and without which no man can answer for the salutary effect of any abstract plan of government or of freedom. For want of these, they have seen the medicine of the state corrupted into its poison. They have seen the French rebel against a mild and lawful monarch, with more fury, outrage, and insult, than ever any people has been known to rise against the most illegal usurper, or the most sanguinary tyrant. Their resistance was made to concession; their revolt was from protection; their blow was aimed at a hand holding out graces, favours, and immunities.

This was unnatural. The rest is in order. They have found their punishment in their success. Laws overturned; tribunals subverted; industry without vigour; commerce expiring; the revenue unpaid, yet the people impoverished; a church pillaged, and a state not relieved; civil and military anarchy made the constitution of the kingdom; everything human and divine sacrificed to the idol of public credit, and national bankruptcy the consequence; and, to crown all, the paper securities of new, precarious, tottering power, the discredited paper securities of impoverished fraud, and beggared rapine, held out as a currency for the support of the empire, in lieu of the two great recognized species that represent the lasting, conventional credit of mankind, which disappeared and hid themselves in the earth from whence they came, when the principle of property, whose creatures and representatives they are, was systematically subverted.

Were all these dreadful things necessary? Were they the inevitable results of the desperate struggle of determined patriots, compelled to wade through blood and tumult, to the quiet shore of a tranquil and prosperous liberty? No! nothing like it. The fresh ruins of France, which shock our feelings wherever we can turn our eyes, are not the devastation of civil war; they are the sad but instructive monuments of rash and ignorant counsel in time of profound peace. They are the display of inconsiderate and presumptuous, because unresisted and irresistible authority. The persons who have thus squandered away the precious treasure of their crimes, the persons who have made this prodigal and wild waste of public evils (the last stake reserved for the ultimate ransom of the state) have met in their progress with little, or rather with no opposition at all. Their whole march was more like a triumphal procession, than the progress of a war. Their pioneers have gone before them, and demolished and laid everything level at their feet. Not one drop of *their* blood have they shed in the cause of the country they have ruined. They have made no sacrifices to their projects of greater consequence than their shoebuckles, whilst they were imprisoning their king, murdering their fellow-citizens, and bathing in tears, and plunging in poverty and distress, thousands of worthy men and worthy families. Their cruelty has not even been the base result of fear. It has been the effect of their sense of perfect safety, in authorizing treasons, robberies, rapes, assassinations, slaughters, and burnings, throughout their harassed land. But the cause of all was plain from the beginning.

Edmund Burke, "Reflections on the Revolution in France, and on the Proceedings in Certain Societies in London Relative to That Event: in a Letter Intended to Have Been Sent to a Gentleman in Paris," in *The Works of the Right Honourable Edmund Burke*, with an introduction by F.W. Raffety. London: Oxford University Press, 1907. Reprinted 1934, vol. 4, pp. 41–43.

Document 16: A Denial of the Inferiority of Women

Mary Wollstonecraft (1759–1797), a radical and dedicated English feminist, is best known for her seminal work, A Vindication of the Rights of Woman, *published in 1792. Arguing at length that women have been op-*

pressed, constricted, subjugated, and degraded by men throughout the ages on the grounds of their supposed inferiority, she calls for a revolution in the treatment and education of women, as can be seen in the following passages.

Do passive indolent women make the best wives? Confining our discussion to the present moment of existence, let us see how such weak creatures perform their part? Do the women who, by the attainment of a few superficial accomplishments, have strengthened the prevailing prejudice, merely contribute to the happiness of their husbands? Do they display their charms merely to amuse them? And have women who have early imbibed notions of passive obedience, sufficient character to manage a family or educate children? So far from it, that, after surveying the history of woman, I cannot help agreeing with the severest satirist, considering the sex as the weakest as well as the most oppressed half of the species. What does history disclose but marks of inferiority, and how few women have emancipated themselves from the galling yoke of sovereign man? . . .

As to the argument respecting the subjection in which the sex has ever been held, it retorts on man. The many have always been enthralled by the few; and monsters, who scarcely have shown any discernment of human excellence, have tyrannized over thousands of their fellow-creatures. Why have men of superior endowments submitted to such degradation? For, is it not universally acknowledged that kings, viewed collectively, have ever been inferior, in abilities and virtue, to the same number of men taken from the common mass of mankind—yet have they not, and are they not still treated with a degree of reverence that is an insult to reason? China is not the only country where a living man has been made a God. *Men* have submitted to superior strength to enjoy with impunity the pleasure of the moment; *women* have only done the same, and therefore till it is proved that the courtier, who servilely resigns the birthright of a man, is not a moral agent, it cannot be demonstrated that woman is essentially inferior to man because she has always been subjugated.

Mary Wollstonecraft, *Vindication of the Rights of Woman*, ed. Miriam Brody. London: Penguin, 1975, pp. 119, 122.

Document 17: *The Rights of Woman*

Marie Olympe Aubrey de Gouges, also known as Marie Gouze (1748–1793), was a French contemporary of Mary Wollstonecraft and, like the Englishwoman, was a radical feminist fighting for woman's rights. In The Rights of Woman, *published in 1791 and excerpted below, Gouges argues that the benefits of the revolution in France must accrue to women no less than to men. She asserts quite unequivocally that woman is man's equal and thus entitled to the same rights, privileges, and civic duties.*

Man, are you capable of justice? The question is being put to you by a woman; and you will at least not deny her the right to do this. Tell me. What has given you the sovereign right to oppress my sex? Your strength? Your talents? Observe the creator in all his wisdom; look at nature in all its grandeur, to which it seems you want to be close, and give me an example, if you dare, of such tyrannical control as this.[1]

Go back to the animals, consult the elements, study the plants and then cast your eyes over all the different varieties of organised matter; yield to the evidence when I give you the means to do so. Seek out, inspect and distinguish, if you can, the sexes in the workings of nature. Everywhere you will find them merged; everywhere they work together as a harmonious whole within this immortal work of art.

Only man has concocted some dreadful principle out of being the exception to this. Bizarre, blind, puffed up by science and, in this century of enlightenment and wisdom, having fallen into the crassest state of ignorance, he wants to rule like a despot over a sex endowed with all the faculties of the intellect. . . .

Postscript

Women, wake up! The alarm-bells of reason can be heard all over the world. Recognise your rights. The powerful rule of nature is no longer hemmed in by prejudices, fanaticism, superstition and lies. The torch of truth has dispelled the clouds of foolishness and usurpation. Man enslaved has doubled his efforts, and [still] needed yours to break his chains. Now that he is free, he has become unjust towards his companion. Oh Women! Women! When will your blindness end? What advantages have you gained from the Revolution? A more marked distrust, a more obvious contempt. In the centuries of corruption you have reigned only over man's weakness. Your little empire has been destroyed; so what do you have left? The proof of man's injustices.

Marie Olympe Aubrey de Gouges, *The Rights of Women*, ed. O. Blanc, in *The Enlightenment*, ed. David Williams. Cambridge, UK: Cambridge University Press, 1999, pp. 318–23.

Document 18: Rousseau Abandons His Children

Among the influential writings of Jean-Jacques Rousseau (1712–1778) is his great autobiographical work The Confessions, *completed in 1765*

---

1. From Paris to Peru, from Japan to Rome, in my opinion the stupidest animal is Man. [*Note by Gouges.*]

and published posthumously in 1781. Rousseau does more than recount the events of his life. His detailed descriptions of his childhood, his feelings, his self-absorption, and his prolonged bitter unhappiness are combined with brutally frank revelations about what is generally taken to be shameful behavior. One such instance, concerning the children born of his relationship with Thérèse Le Vasseur, is his abandonment of these children, each of whom he placed in an orphanage so that the state would pay for their upbringing. Rousseau's explanation of his actions is set forth in the following excerpt from The Confessions.

Whilst I was philosophizing on the duties of man an event occurred which made me reflect more deeply upon my own. Thérèse [Le Vasseur] became pregnant for the third time. Too sincere with myself, too proud in my heart, to be willing to belie my principles by my actions, I began to consider the fate of my children and my relationship with their mother, by reference to the laws of nature, justice, and reason. . . .

If I was mistaken in my conclusions, nothing can be more remarkable than the calm spirit in which I surrendered to them. If I were one of those low-born men, deaf to the gentle voice of Nature, a man in whose breast no real feeling of justice and humanity ever arose, this hardness of heart would have been quite easy to explain. But my warm-heartedness, my acute sensibility, the ease with which I formed friendships, the hold they exercised over me, and the cruel wrench when they had to be broken; my innate goodwill towards my fellow men; my burning love for the great, the true, the beautiful, and the just; my horror of evil in every form, my inability to hate, to hurt, or even to wish to; that softening, that sharp and sweet emotion I feel at the sight of all that is virtuous, generous, and lovable: is it possible that all these can ever dwell in the same soul along with depravity which, quite unscrupulously, tramples the dearest of obligations underfoot? No, I feel, and boldly declare—it is impossible. Never for a moment in his life could Jean-Jacques have been a man without feelings or compassion, an unnatural father. I may have been mistaken, but I could never be callous. If I were to state my reasons, I should say too much. For since they were strong enough to seduce me, they would seduce many others; and I do not wish to expose any young people who may read me to the risk of being misled by the same error. I will be content with a general statement that in handing my children over for the State to educate, for lack of means to bring them up myself, by destining them to become workers and peasants instead of adventurers and fortune-hunters, I thought I was acting as a citizen and a father, and looked upon myself as a member of Plato's Republic. More than once since then the regret in my heart has told me that I was wrong. But far from my reason having told me the same story, I have often blessed Heaven for having thus safeguarded them from their father's fate, and from that which would have overtaken them at the moment when I should have been compelled to abandon them. . . .

My third child, therefore was taken to the Foundling Hospital like the others, and the next two were disposed of in the same way, for I had five in all. This arrangement seemed so good and sensible and right to me that if I did not boast of it openly it was solely out of regard for their mother. But I told everyone whom I had told of our relationship . . . and this freely, frankly, and under no kind of compulsion, at a time when I might easily have concealed the matter from everybody. . . . In a word, I made no mystery about my conduct, not only because I have never been able to conceal anything from my friends, but because I really saw nothing wrong in it. All things considered, I made the best choice for my children, or what I thought was the best. I could have wished, and still do wish, that I had been brought up and nurtured as they have been.

Jean-Jacques Rousseau, *The Confessions*, trans. J.M. Cohen. London: Penguin, 1953, pp. 332–34.

Document 19: Voltaire's Contempt for Rousseau

François-Marie Arouet de Voltaire (1694–1778) and Jean-Jacques Rousseau, the two most eminent of the philosophes, *were initially friends who admired each other. Gradually, however, as they disagreed on various issues, their relationship deteriorated into one of mutual enmity. Voltaire openly criticized Rousseau and, in the following letter to a fellow* philosophe, Jean le Rond D'Alembert *(a mathematician and coeditor of the* Encyclopedia), *he reveals the extent of his contempt for Rousseau.*

To Jean Le Rond D'Alembert. June 17, 1762.

Excessive pride and envy have destroyed Jean-Jacques, my illustrious philosopher. That monster dares speak of education! A man who refused to raise any of his sons and put them all in foundling homes! He abandoned his children and the tramp [Thérèse Le Vasseur] with whom he made them. He has only failed to write against his tramp as he has written against his friends. . . . I do not know whether he is abhorred in Paris as he is by all the upright people of Geneva.

François-Marie Arouet de Voltaire, letter to Jean le Rond d'Alembert, 17 June 1762, trans. and ed. Richard A. Brooks, in *Rousseau's Political Writings*, ed. Alan Ritter and Julia Conaway Bondanella. New York: W.W. Norton, 1988, p. 194.

Discussion Questions

Chapter 1

1. Referring to the articles by Norman Hampson and Jonathan I. Israel, discuss the most important aspects of the seventeenth-century worldview.

2. Contrast early-seventeenth-century views about the universe to those of eighteenth-century science using Hampson's article as a reference.

3. According to Israel, why was traditional religious philosophy superseded by Enlightenment thought?

4. Describe the tripartite battle of ideas in the early Enlightenment and explain its significance as indicated by Israel.

5. Explain how the prevailing view of women in seventeenth-century Europe was based on what Phyllis Mack terms "feminine symbols and stereotypes." Why were there two conflicting images of women? How were superstitions about women related to the religious beliefs of the time? Show how attitudes to women changed in the eighteenth century.

Chapter 2

1. Analyze Montesquieu's concept of "natural law." Explain Montesquieu's reasons for arguing that the different laws of various countries are all based on natural law.

2. Locke and Rousseau both assume that human beings lived in a state of nature prior to civilization. What kind of arguments does each use to support this assumption? Compare and contrast their views on the state of nature as well as on the social contract, as set forth by D.J. O'Connor and Bertrand Russell. How do their descriptions of the state of nature differ from the biblical account of the Garden of Eden?

3. On what grounds does Russell criticize Rousseau's concept of a democratic state in which all citizens surrender their individual rights for the greater good? Assess the arguments that Russell uses to warn of the dangers inherent in Rousseau's theory.

4. Explain Pauline Maier's statement that "revolution did not necessarily imply republicanism." Define the term *republicanism* and

discuss its characteristics. Why did the colonists not choose some version of monarchy?

5. Referring to the articles by Maier and Frederick M. Watkins, discuss the points of similarity and contrast between the American and the French revolutions. Why did both revolutions repudiate the divine right of kings? How did each revolution embody Enlightenment ideals?

Chapter 3

1. Trace the historical origins of the scientific method popularized by the *philosophes*, as discussed by Frank E. Manuel. Specify the contributions of individual thinkers and philosophers.

2. Roy Porter asks the question: Were the *philosophes* responsible for causing the French Revolution? What answer does he give? Explain why you agree or disagree with Porter.

3. Explain what Peter Gay means when he says that "the reign of fact" replaced "the reign of fancy." Why did the *philosophes* repudiate religion and turn instead to science?

4. With reference to the articles in this chapter, discuss the definitive characteristics of the new scientific method that prevailed in the Enlightenment. Specify the advantages of the scientific method over religious disputation. Analyze some of the notable achievements of the scientific method.

Chapter 4

1. Describe the respective political aims of the conservative majority and the progressive minority in late-eighteenth-century Europe as indicated by Leonard Krieger. To what extent did economic and demographic factors affect the changes that were occurring?

2. According to Diana H. Coole, how does Rousseau differentiate between the roles assigned to men and to women in his vision of society? What justification does he provide for this differentiation of roles? What is the function of the patriarchal family in Rousseau's concept of society? Analyze critically Rousseau's view that the "natural" qualities of women must be carefully "nurtured." On what grounds does Rousseau argue that women should not be considered citizens? Why, then, does he consider women indispensable to society? Why do Coole and other feminist historians consider Rousseau's views about women offensive?

3. How does Susan P. Conner define the term *political influence*? Explain the different kinds of political influence exerted by women in eighteenth-century France. Why do feminists feel contempt for the role played by aristocratic women at court?

4. Citing the essay by Jean Starobinski, analyze the validity of the *philosophes'* assertions: first, that the concept of civilization implied its opposite—a primordial original state; second, that civilization implied various stages in the evolution of mankind. To what extent did the voyages of discovery provide evidence for these assertions by the *philosophes*? Why did some *philosophes* regard civilized manners as hypocritical?

Chapter 5

1. According to Claire G. Moses, what feminist ideals did French-women strive to achieve during the Enlightenment? Why did women in the eighteenth century fail to achieve them? Explain how the seeds sown in the Enlightenment bore fruit in the twentieth century for French feminists.

2. Explain why Ira O. Wade maintains that the Enlightenment belief in optimism, progress, liberty, and equality was made possible only by repudiating the authority of church and king. Give reasons why you agree or disagree with Wade's assertion that the teachings of three of the *philosophes* comprise the legacy of the Enlightenment.

General

1. How did the *philosophes* undermine the power of the *ancien régime* in France? What impact did they have on European and American history?

2. During the Enlightenment, secular thought prevailed over religious doctrine. In your opinion, has this been beneficial or detrimental to European progress? Explain why you have come to this conclusion?

3. What are the most significant achievements of the eighteenth-century Enlightenment? Why is the Enlightenment considered a turning point in history?

4. Explain why the Enlightenment has been described as an era in which the light of reason and knowledge illuminated the darkness of superstition and ignorance.

Chronology

1688
Glorious Revolution in England: abdication of Catholic monarch James II and accession to the throne by Protestants William and Mary of Orange.

1689
Birth of Charles-Louis de Secondat de Montesquieu.

1690
John Locke's *Two Treatises on Government* published.

1694
Birth of François-Marie Arouet de Voltaire.

1712
Birth of Jean-Jacques Rousseau.

1713
Birth of Denis Diderot.

1714–1727
Reign of George I of England.

1715
Death of Louis XIV of France.

1715–1774
Reign of Louis XV of France.

1721
Montesquieu's *Persian Letters* published.

1727–1760
Reign of George II of England.

1740–1780
Reign of Maria Theresa of Austria.

1740–1786
Reign of Frederick II (the Great) of Prussia.

1748
Publication of Montesquieu's *The Spirit of the Laws* and David Hume's *Inquiry Concerning Human Understanding*.

1751–1772
Publication of twenty-eight volumes of the *Encyclopedia*, edited by Diderot.

1755
Death of Montesquieu.

1759
Voltaire's *Candide* published

1760–1820
Reign of George III of England.

1762
Rousseau's *The Social Contract* and *Émile* published.

1762–1769
Reign of Catherine II (the Great) of Russia.

1764
Publication of Cesare Bonesana Beccaria's *On Crimes and Punishments*.

1774–1793
Reign of Louis XVI of France.

1776
American Declaration of Independence and the American Revolution; publication of Adam Smith's *Inquiry into the Nature and Causes of the Wealth of Nations*.

1778
Death of Rousseau and Voltaire.

1780–1790
Reign of Joseph II of Austria.

1781
Joseph II's decree emancipating the serfs and his Edict of Toleration for Protestants; Immanuel Kant's *Critique of Pure Reason* published.

1782
Joseph II's Edict of Toleration for Jews; posthumous publication of first six volumes of Rousseau's *Confessions*.

1784
Death of Diderot.

1789

Proclamation in France of the *Declaration of the Rights of Man and of the Citizen* and the French Revolution.

1791

Thomas Paine's *Rights of Man* published.

1792

Mary Wollstonecraft's *A Vindication of the Rights of Woman* published.

For Further Research

Reference Works

Jeremy Black and Roy Porter, eds., *The Basic Blackwell Dictionary of World Eighteenth-Century History.* Oxford: Blackwell, 1994.

John W. Yolton, ed., *The Blackwell Companion to the Enlightenment.* Oxford: Blackwell, 1991.

Collections of Original Documents of the Enlightenment

Lewis White Beck, ed., *Eighteenth-Century Philosophy.* New York: The Free Press, 1966.

Crane Brinton, ed., *The Portable Age of Reason Reader.* New York: Viking, 1956.

Lester G. Crocker, ed., *The Age of Enlightenment.* New York: Harper, 1969.

Peter Gay, ed., *The Enlightenment.* New York: Simon & Schuster, 1973.

Isaac Kramnick, ed., *The Portable Enlightenment Reader.* New York: Penguin, 1995.

Leonard M. Marsdak, ed., *The Enlightenment.* New York: John Wiley & Sons, 1972.

Alan Ritter and Julia Conaway Bondanella, eds., *Rousseau's Political Writings: Discourse on Inequality, Discourse on Political Economy, On Social Contract.* New York: W.W. Norton, 1988.

James Schmidt, ed., *What Is Enlightenment? Eighteenth-Century Answers and Twentieth-Century Questions.* Berkeley: University of California Press, 1996.

David Williams, ed., *The Enlightenment.* Cambridge, UK: Cambridge University Press, 1999.

———, *Voltaire: Political Writings.* Cambridge, UK: Cambridge University Press, 1994.

David Wooton, ed., *Modern Political Thought: Readings from Machiavelli to Nietzsche.* Indianapolis: Hackett, 1996.

General Studies of the Enlightenment

Robert Anchor, *The Enlightenment Tradition*. 1967. Reprinted Berkeley: University of California Press, 1979.

Peter Gay, *The Enlightenment: An Interpretation*. 2 vols. New York: Vintage, 1966–1969.

Norman Hampson, *The Enlightenment*. Harmondsworth, UK: Penguin, 1968.

Daniel Roche, *France in the Enlightenment*. Cambridge, MA: Harvard University Press, 1998.

Ira O. Wade, *The Structure and Form of the French Enlightenment*. 2 vols. Princeton, NJ: Princeton University Press, 1977.

The Political Context of the Enlightenment

T.C. Blanning, *The French Revolution: Artistocrats Versus Bourgeois?* London: Macmillan, 1987.

Maurice Cranston, *Philosophers and Pamphleteers: Political Theorists of the Enlightenment*. Oxford: Oxford University Press, 1986.

Leo Gershoy, *From Despotism to Revolution, 1763–1789*. New York: Harper & Row, 1963.

Leonard Krieger, *Kings and Philosophers, 1689–1789*. New York: W.W. Norton, 1970.

Walter Oppenheim, *Europe and the Enlightened Despots*. London: Hodder & Stoughton, 1990.

Roy Porter, *Enlightenment: Britain and the Creation of the Modern World*. Harmondsworth, UK: Penguin, 2000.

R.J. White, *Europe in the Eighteenth Century*. New York: St. Martin's, 1965.

America and the Enlightenment

Bernard Bailyn, *The Ideological Origins of the American Revolution*. Cambridge, MA: Harvard University Press, Belknap Press, 1967.

Henry F. May, *The Enlightenment in America*. New York: Oxford University Press, 1976.

Gary Wills, *Inventing America: Jefferson's Declaration of Independence*. Garden City, NY: Doubleday, 1978.

Enlightenment Philosophy and Intellectual History

S.C. Brown, ed., *Philosophers of the Enlightenment*. Brighton, UK: Harvester, 1979.

Ernst Cassirer, *The Philosophy of the Enlightenment*. Trans. Fritz C.A. Koellen and James Pettegrove. Boston: Beacon, 1964.

Paul Hazard, *The European Mind, 1680–1715*. Cleveland: Meridian, 1963.

———, *European Thought in the Eighteenth Century: From Montesquieu to Lessing*. Cleveland: Meridian, 1963.

Jonathan I. Israel, *Radical Enlightenment: Philosophy and the Making of Modernity 1650–1750*. Oxford: Oxford University Press, 2001.

A.C. Kors and Paul J. Korshin, eds., *Anticipations of the Enlightenment in England, France, and Germany*. Philadephia: University of Pennsylvania Press, 1987.

David Spadafora, *The Idea of Progress in Eighteenth Century Britain*. New Haven, CT: Yale University Press, 1990.

Ira O. Wade, *The Intellectual Origins of the French Enlightenment*. Princeton, NJ: Princeton University Press, 1971.

Earl R. Wasserman, ed., *Aspects of the Eighteenth Century*. Baltimore: Johns Hopkins University Press, 1965.

R.J. White, *The Anti-Philosophers: A Study of the Philosophes in Eighteenth-Century France*. London: Macmillan, 1970.

Religion in Enlightenment Europe

James Byrne, *Glory, Jest and Riddle: Religious Thought in the Enlightenment*. London: SCM Press, 1996.

Marijke Gijswijt-Hofstra, Brian P. Levack, and Roy Porter, *Witchcraft and Magic in Europe*. Vol. 5: *The Eighteenth and Nineteenth Centuries*. London: Athlone, 1999.

Ole Peter Grell and Roy Porter, eds., *Toleration in Enlightenment Europe*. Cambridge, UK: Cambridge University Press, 2000.

Frank E. Manuel, *The Eighteenth Century Confronts the Gods*. New York: Atheneum, 1967.

Social and Cultural Contexts of the Enlightenment

C.B.A. Behrens, *The Ancien Régime*. London: Thames and Hudson, 1967.

W. Doyle, *The Ancien Régime*. London: Macmillan, 1986.

Franklin L. Ford, *Robe and Sword: The Regrouping of the French Aristocracy After Louis XIV.* Cambridge, MA: Harvard University Press, 1953.

Dena Goodman, *The Republic of Letters: A Cultural History of the French Enlightenment.* Ithaca, NY: Cornell University Press, 1994.

Margaret Hunt et al., *Women in the Enlightenment.* New York: Haworth Press, 1984.

John Lough, *An Introduction to Eighteenth-Century France.* London: Longmans, Green, 1960.

Samia I. Spencer, ed., *French Women and the Age of Enlightenment.* Bloomington: Indiana University Press, 1984.

Science and the Social Sciences in the Enlightenment

William Clark, Jan Golinski, and Simon Schaffer, eds., *The Sciences in Enlightened Europe.* Chicago: University of Chicago Press, 1999.

Christopher Fox, Roy Porter, and Robert Wokler, eds., *Inventing Human Science: Eighteenth Century Domains.* Berkeley: University of California Press, 1995.

Thomas L. Hankins, *Science and the Enlightenment.* Cambridge, UK, and New York: Cambridge University Press, 1985.

Richard Olson, *The Emergence of the Social Sciences, 1642–1792.* New York: Twayne, 1993.

Roy Porter, ed., *The Cambridge History of Science.* Vol. 4: *The Eighteenth Century.* Cambridge, UK: Cambridge University Press, 2000.

G.S. Rousseau and Roy Porter, eds., *The Ferment of Knowledge: Studies in the Historiography of Eighteenth Century Science.* Cambridge, UK: Cambridge University Press, 1980.

Studies of Major Enlightenment Figures

Gregory Claey, *Thomas Paine: Social and Political Thought.* Winchester, MA: Unwin Hyman, 1989.

Alfred Cobban, *Edmund Burke and the Revolt Against the Eighteenth Century.* 2nd ed. New York: Barnes & Noble, 1960.

Maurice Cranston, *Jean-Jacques: The Early Life and Work of Jean-Jacques Rousseau.* London: Allen Lane, 1983.

Maurice Cranston and Richard Peters, eds., *Hobbes and Rousseau: A Collection of Critical Essays*, Garden City, NY: Doubleday, 1972.

Peter Gay, *Voltaire's Politics: The Poet as Realist.* 1956. Reprinted New Haven, CT: Yale University Press, 1988.

John C. Hall, *Rousseau: An Introduction to His Political Philosophy.* London: Macmillan, 1973.

J. Keane, *Tom Paine: A Political Life.* London: Bloomsbury, 1996.

Hugh Mason, *Voltaire: A Biography.* Baltimore, MD: Johns Hopkins University Press, 1981.

James Miller, *Rousseau: Dreamer of Democracy.* New Haven, CT: Yale University Press, 1984.

Susan Moller Okin, *Rousseau.* Part III of *Women in Western Political Thought.* Princeton, NJ: Princeton University Press, 1979.

Peter Schouls, *Reasoned Freedom: John Locke and Enlightenment.* Ithaca, NY: Cornell University Press, 1992.

Robert Shackleton, *Montesquieu: A Critical Biography.* Oxford: Clarendon Press, 1961.

Judith N. Shklar, *Men and Citizens: A Study of Rousseau's Social Theory.* Cambridge, UK: Cambridge University Press, 1969.

———, *Montesquieu.* Oxford: Oxford University Press, 1987.

D.A. Lloyd Thomas, *Locke on Government.* London: Routledge, 1995.

Arthur Wilson, *Diderot: The Testing Years, 1713–1759.* New York: Oxford University Press, 1969.

Index

absolute monarchy. *See* monarchy
agrarian societies, 118–19, 122
Alembert, Jean d', 8, 93, 110
American colonists
  goals of, 72
  rejection of monarchy by, 74–77
  republicanism and, 72–74, 77
American Revolution (1776), 12, 72
  compared with French Revolution, 80–81
  consensus for, 84
  Paine's involvement in, 79–80
Amsterdam, 123
Arouet, François-Marie. *See* Voltaire
astronomy, 27

Bacon, Francis, 93, 95–96
Beck, Lewis White, 9
Bentham, Jeremy, 100
Bible, the
  authority of, 19, 21–22
  discrepancies in, 94–95
birthrate, 121–22
Bondanella, Julia Conaway, 67
Bossuet, Jacques-Benigne, 20, 26, 101–102
Browne, Thomas, 25
Brumfitt, J.H., 53
Burke, Edmund, 99–100

Cartesian rationalism, 56, 94
Catholic Church, 9
  see also Christian churches/ Christianity
Chambers, Ephraim, 108
Christian churches/Christianity
  attack on, by *philosophes*, 9, 97–98
  challenged by the intelligentsia, 10–11, 12
  classical learning and, 19–21
  divisions within, 43
  before and after 1650, 36–37
civilization
  artificial politeness and, 144–45
  barbarity and, 142–43, 143–44
  as an ideal, 143
  as a process, 141

classical learning, 19–21
Condillac, Etienne de, 96
confessional antagonism, age of, 39
Conner, Susan P., 135
Coole, Diana H., 127
Copernicus, Nicolaus, 27
Counter-Enlightenment, 39
Cyclopedia (Chambers), 108

death rate, 121
Decline and Fall of the Roman Empire (Gibbons), 102
democracy
  French Revolution and, 85–86
  French revolutionary ideology and, 81–82
  Locke's political theory and, 49–50
  Rousseau on, 63–64, 70
  Secondat on, 57, 58–59
democratic republicanism, 44
Descartes, René, 93, 94
despotism, 57, 58, 59
dictatorship, French Revolution and, 85–86
Diderot, Denis, 9, 93, 158
  contribution of, 161–62
  on experience, 95
  on nature, 107–109, 110–11
  on reason, 94

economic/social life
  changes in, 118–21
  corporate institutions and, 117–18
  differences in growth of European countries and, 124–25
  industrialization and, 125–26
  international trade and, 122–24
  population growth's impact on, 121–22
  social classes and, 80–81, 118–19
education
  childhood, Rousseau on, 67
  for women, 152, 154
eighteenth century
  repression of women at end of, 150
  revolutionary ferment in France

199